ESSENTIAL HANDBOOKS
FOR CHRISTIANS

THE PROCESS

OF THE PROPHETIC

VOL.

II

ANDREW BILLINGS

WITH A FOREWORD BY: DAVID HOGAN

CONTENTS

FOREWORD

I believe that our walk with God is a journey. In the journey, we are processing, walking, living and praising God. I believe in this walk (this journey). I believe in this man's walk. I believe in this man's family. And I believe in this man's God. Jesus is King!

—David L. Hogan

INTRODUCTION

The peak, which is the most climactic point, of the purpose of our existence is to embrace the face and voice of God. It is to be known by Him and to know Him; to hear His voice and to be absorbed by His golden, molten love that melts away space for anything else but His goodness and loving nature. The more we get to know God as a father and a friend, becoming acquainted with His presence, the more we want to meet with Him each day.

Are you ready to progress further and deeper in your walk into all of who God is? He is calling you by name to respond and venture out beyond where you are comfortable, into places in Him that only your hunger and desperation can take you. God desires to reveal His mysteries and show you His secrets that are only reserved for His lovers. He is calling you to learn and become familiar with His voice. He wants to show you His heart and give understanding so you can better see and perceive His plans and desires, His will and His ways.

Now that you have read through volume one of The Guild of the Prophets, *The Foundations of the Prophetic*, you have been equipped to go deeper into the prophetic realm. This second book excites me;

I have an anticipation for you to connect with the voice and heart of God in ways you have not yet known. He is calling you to incline your ear to His whispers. For many of us, we are unsure how to do that. We may ask, "How do I become intimate with God and learn to hear His voice? How do I understand what God is doing? How do God's promises work?" Here is where we start. This volume is going to take you on a journey that will answer these questions, equipping you with the ability to hear and understand the voice and heart of God, in both your life and in the lives of those around you.

My personal journey in hearing the voice of God has been one of desperation and longing. I was desperate to hear God's voice for myself, and to know that it was really Him I was hearing. It took me a while, but gradually I became acquainted with His voice. I am still learning because I want to maintain a teachable spirit, and I will learn for the rest of my life, growing in my understanding of the ways of God, His wisdom, and the timing in which He reveals promises and callings. One of the keys we are going to grasp is understanding God's heart and His perspective in the outworking and the timing of His plans for our lives.

This volume is focused on training you how to follow God's process by hearing and discerning His voice, how to walk out God's instructions, and how to inherit God's promises. It's important you learn to do this well before you attempt to minister and influence others with your prophetic gift. Enjoy this process of learning. Your personal relationship with God is more important than any ministry you can have or do. To minister in the prophetic realm, you must exhibit credible fruit, and show maturity in the principles raised in this book. When your personal life reflects these principles and produces desirable fruits, others will want to receive from you.

Position your heart to receive. I pray that you will have life-changing encounters with the Spirit of the Lord as you read the second volume for The Guild of the Prophets—*The Process of the Prophetic.*

—Andrew Billings

CHAPTER 1

UNDERSTANDING GOD'S HEART AND LOVE TOWARD YOU

Life is a wonderful gift, full of hopes, dreams, and expectations. On the other end of the spectrum, however, life also has challenging seasons of wondering and waiting. There are seasons of extended delays, and even extreme challenges on the path as God's promises come about. Understanding the heart of God in your journey will help bring perspective and a correct interpretation of God's plans as His promises are worked out in your life.

Jeremiah 29:11 records God's heart for you. The blessings and dreams He has in store for you are conscious and intentional. "For I know the thoughts that I think toward you, says the LORD, thoughts of peace and not of evil, to give you a future and a hope." And God instructs us in Habakkuk 2:2–3 (NIV):

Then the LORD replied:

"Write down the revelation and make it plain on tablets so that a herald may run with it. For the revelation awaits an appointed time; it speaks of the end and will not prove false. Though it linger, wait for it; it will certainly come and will not delay."

God has a ridiculously generous, abundant dream over your life's journey. After all, He is the author and finisher of your story. But a disconnect from God often comes when people do not understand delays or the seasons that God arranges between the promise and the realization of the vision. We often interpret a perceived delay as a rejection from God or a self-induced failure that has caused God to withdraw His blessing or promise from us. This feeling of disconnect is often not a reality, and it is certainly nothing close to the goodness or kindness of God's nature.

It can be difficult when people feel that God has not answered or brought about a promise in the time they expected it would come. Prophetic people can find this God-timing even more challenging than most. As prophetic people who are learning or who are in tune to this part of God's nature, we will often see or hear God's promises and perceive them through the eyes of faith that sees the promise "as though it were here, right now" (see Romans 4:17 KJV). In other words, we can find ourselves saying, "Why hasn't it happened yet? I can see it with my faith, and now I don't understand why it isn't in my present." Walking out promises will require us to know God, not just know *about* Him.

The writer of Hebrews says, "But without faith it is impossible to please him: for he that cometh to God must believe that he is, and that he is a rewarder of them that diligently seek him" (Hebrews 11:6 KJV). There is so much here as we look closer at this scripture: "... for he that cometh to God must believe that He is ..." We must believe that God exists, but there is more to it than that. God is the embodiment and the very expression of love. We must believe and soundly grasp that all God decrees and speaks is motivated by love, even when we don't understand it, when there are delays, or it is corrective in nature. Believing this is fundamental to walking out the promises we receive from our Father.

One of the great issues facing our generation is that we are used to instant service, fast and faster results. But God is a God of the old paths; His ways remain constant, not stagnant. This "entitlement mentality" is a cancer in today's society. Yes, we are God's children and our faith does obtain promises; however, "love is patient and kind ... it does not demand its own way" (1 Corinthians 13:4–5 NLT).

If we look at the earth today, it is mainly separated into countries that are either democratically, socialistically, or communistically ruled. There are few that are classed as a kingdom in which a king solely has supreme rule. The kingdom of heaven is ruled by a King— our God and Father. Understanding that even though we are the apple of God's eye and His affection, the universe does not revolve around us. Rather, the universe revolves around God and is ruled by Him. Behaving badly when something hasn't arrived when we expected it to, is not walking in love or honor; rather, it is acting out of an entitlement mentality.

Understanding that God is love is fundamental to this process of walking out His promises. He only wants what's best for us, but He would never give us something before we are ready for it because it would damage us. He is such a wise Father. For example, I love my three sons—much more than all my descriptive abilities could ever pen, but that love is tempered with wisdom. I would never purchase a car for them to drive while they are little children. Driving a vehicle without maturity and guidance would be catastrophic to their well-being. I put them on my lap in our Suburban and let them pretend to steer the car while we sit in our garage, giving them a small taste and a glimpse of their future. They love it. They get excited because they are emulating my behavior.

God is very much the same with us. We have moments where God reveals small glimpses to us of our destiny and future. We taste where He is taking us. We sit on His lap and hold the steering wheel and get excited, thinking we are about to immediately launch into our new season. And then nothing happens. We begin to question in our minds, wondering if we missed it or if God forgot about us. We didn't miss it, and God hasn't forgotten one word of His promises toward us. Rather, He is taking us through a season.

Hebrews advises us here:

> "Looking unto Jesus, the author and finisher of our faith, who for the joy that was set before Him endured the cross, despising the shame, and has sat down at the right hand of the throne of God" (Hebrews 12:2).

If you grasp this passage and understand that God is for you and not against you, then you will be able to endure the seasons when promises are not arriving at the time you expected. You will be able to trust God's judgment over your own discomfort as your dreams and promises seem unfairly delayed.

In God's wisdom, He shares a glimpse of the destination, but rarely does He promise the timing of the fulfillment of the promise. Without maintaining hope, we would perish or waste away in our hearts. God understands this, so He gives us pointers to guide us into the direction He is taking us.

God values the journey more than the destination. It is the journey that prepares, equips, and even qualifies us for the destination to which God is taking us. The endurance, faithfulness, resolve, and determination to walk in faith are all unique to each of us. God's desire is that we gain strength of spirit while we are being prepared for the fulfillment of the promised destiny.

It is wise to be conscious and attentive about this. Our dreams and wants need to be in alignment with God's. We must not be hasty to want it before we are ready for it. The process is the period between the promise and that promise materializing. It is such a valuable time, even when we think it's extended or extremely uncomfortable.

God's heart is so generous, abundantly loving, compassionate, and wise toward us that He wants what is best for us. In getting us to the best—to His plans and purposes—we must go through an equipping process to be able to walk in and hold the promises He intended for us. It's almost as if the journey is a response to the invitation of the promise. The promise is the motivation we need to move us toward the place of God's intended grand design.

The trouble is that when God speaks to us and reveals our destiny and purpose He is often speaking of a conditional future. He is inviting us into something that awakens our hearts but we are likely not ready for it. In His amazing wisdom, the Father understands that the challenges, obstacles, environment, pressures, resistance, and even our own mistakes, will cause us to develop, change, learn, grow, and become equipped along the journey.

You will be in this amazing process of God's fashioning and shaping for the remainder of your life in various ways. Life is a big process, but certain seasons will be defined by sub-journeys. Almost like chapters in a book, a prophetic word can open and commence a new season in our lives in which God begins to hone, refine, and even do surgery in specific areas, overhauling our entire world. The result is that if we walk humbly before God and follow His ways and requirements we will arrive at the right time, prepared, equipped, proven, ready to obtain, and walk in responsibility with maturity in all that God has given. When we choose to see God through the eyes of His love, then we understand His wisdom, leading, and navigation.

God's plans are perfect and will bless us beyond our wildest dreams, if we are prepared to go through the process with patience and attentiveness. We often assess ourselves as far more ready and qualified for the promises than we really are, and we can easily become frustrated when it doesn't happen in the timing we imagined or perceived. The problem is that our imagination often misleads us. The process of His promises, inviting us into His heart's plan for our lives, is a perfectly fine-tuned design that qualifies us on the journey to the destination.

Paul wrote about the fruit of the Spirit in Galatians 5:22–23:

"But the fruit of the Spirit is love, joy, peace, longsuffering, kindness, goodness, faithfulness, gentleness, self-control. Against such there is no law." Our biggest issues here are with control and patience. These are two attributes found in the fruits of the Spirit that we conveniently neglect to exercise in moments of frustration, especially when God hasn't delivered His promise on our schedule. Here we find the key to peace and contentment along our journey, trusting the Master Builder.

One of the greatest principles we can authentically grasp is that God is genuinely the master expert in building lives. He is a genius in design, destiny, and timing. That's why God wants us to stop striving like we know what we are doing, when quite simply we have no clue. We read in the Word of God:

> "But indeed, O man, who are you to reply against God? Will the thing formed say to him who formed it, 'Why have you made me like this?' Does not the potter have power over the clay, from the same lump to make one vessel for honor and another for dishonor?" (Romans 9:20–21).

In other words, we are not in charge of our lives—God is. We get to benefit from His craftsmanship and mentoring, leading us toward amazing destiny and purpose for which He predestined us. However, we don't get all the information up front; we only get to trust. That's why Hebrews 11:6 says that "without faith it's impossible to please God." Trusting God even when we don't understand why circumstances haven't lined up yet, is pleasing to God's heart.

Can you imagine Joseph being disillusioned after having dreams from the Lord? We read in Genesis 37 that he was given *destiny* dreams about his future, yet he had events and seasons during which he was thrown into the pit by his brothers, sold into slavery, falsely accused by Potiphar's wife, and forgotten in prison. All these circumstances spoke the opposite of the promise God had revealed. Yet these were shaping, fashioning, and preparing him for the promise. Joseph became the prime minister of Egypt, second in command only to Pharaoh. When God showed the young man his future, he was not yet ready, mature, or equipped for the task. However, through a journey that most would say was unfair, God's perfect preparation plan was carried out in his life.

We must be careful that we do not murmur and complain along our journey, like the children of Israel did as they travelled from slavery in Egypt to Canaan (see Numbers 11). Even though God had brought them out of slavery and bondage, they were quick to complain. We must learn from their error and not repeat their mistakes.

It has been said that diamonds are formed under incredible pressure. In a process where carbon is compressed, the intense pressure causes diamonds to form. Most people would like to think that diamonds are created in an amazing, miraculous way with no "messy" aspects to it but the truth is that diamonds are formed by an immense pressure that produces a complete metamorphosis. The same is true in our lives.

Just like in Genesis 1 when the earth was without form and void, covered in darkness, and far from even being habitable, God began to speak, creating a habitation where we could live and thrive. God always speaks into what is not yet, as though it was a reality. This is because He is prophesying; He is speaking creative destiny. If we understand that God can create life from what is void, it will make more sense when He speaks to us even when we are not prepared, equipped, or even trained to receive what He promised. He is calling you into your destiny, inviting you on a journey that is almost more important than its destination, where Christ Jesus will be formed in you, and you will become skilled and trained in the areas in which God is calling.

Believing that God's promises are true, prompts His affection, causing Him to entrust us with more revelation. Learning God's heart of love toward us is paramount to our ability to partner with Him. It helps us understand why circumstances happen the way they do. Welcome to the process of the prophetic.

CHAPTER 2

HEARING GOD'S VOICE

One of the defining tests of every prophet is not how accurately he or she can prophesy, predict, foretell, read other people's mail and deliver messages from God, but how well he or she can hear God's voice and be led by His Spirit in his or her personal life. Your gift is not validated by how well and accurately you learn to navigate the gift God has allowed you to use; rather, it is validated by how intimate you are with God. Can you hear God's voice for your own heart and life?

This is one of the great dangers of the prophetic gift. People tend to evaluate their progress and worth as individuals or that of their gifting, by other people's reactions rather than by what God says to them about themselves. When we respond to people's applause, we become "performing prophets" who prophesy for notoriety and attention, rather than humble messengers who are commended by the Father for accurately and faithfully delivering what He said and for giving Him all the glory.

Using your prophetic gift to hear God for others is like operating a well-rehearsed operation. Hearing God's voice, seeing His vision, and being led by His Spirit for your own life does not happen automatically. It happens only through a personal connection and moments of intimacy with God. As I grew in the prophetic, I discovered early on that hearing God for others was very different from hearing God for myself. The practice of the prophetic versus the overflow of intimacy with God are not one and the same. So many prophets go about their lives accurately hearing for others but are bankrupt when hearing God for themselves. It's not just an enchanting gift; it's one that should be walked out with wisdom and discernment and tested by those who receive the word.

Hearing God for yourself is essential not only to the prophet, but to every son and daughter of God. "For as many as are led by the Spirit of God, they are the sons of God" (Romans 8:14). Having the confidence that the voice you heard or the vision you saw is from God, is invaluable. Hearing for yourself is much more assuring than hearing through another person. This will allow you to have undivided focus on what God has said, without wondering about the accuracy of another's message. It is empowering and impactful as well as comforting to know that what you heard or saw was directly from God Himself.

Jesus used the illustration that "His sheep follow him [the shepherd], for they know His voice. Yet they will by no means follow a stranger, but will flee from him, for they do not know the voice of strangers" (John 10:4–5). The good news is that if you are a child of God, then you are qualified to hear God's voice.

HOW DO I HEAR GOD'S VOICE?

God is the embodiment of love, so when He talks to us He is speaking to us from a heart of pure love that wants nothing but the absolute best for our lives. He will speak vision and destiny over you, He will encourage you, and at times He will correct you, but His intention is never to harm you. Rather, His corrective voice only comes to keep you from continuing in the wrong direction or holding to a wrong heart condition so you can ultimately receive the promise. We must meet God in the pursuit of hearing His voice, knowing that He is a good Father. Learning to hear His voice opens us up to His generous heart.

There has been a stigma in much of the church that hearing God's voice is difficult. Hearing God's voice doesn't have to be difficult, however; it is something we must pursue. Hearing God's voice is an important part of our conversation with God, our Maker, Friend, and King. Being able to hear God's responses to our questions and cries is both empowering and satisfying. His voice of correction is calling us to higher levels of character and conduct and may be painful in the moment, but in the end will result in great growth and maturity, Hearing God's voice is the result of following what He told us to do:

"Be still, and know that I am God; I will be exalted among
the nations, I will be exalted in the earth" (Psalm 46:10).

Understanding stillness is a powerful key in the pursuit of God's voice. God speaks to all of us in slightly different ways; however, let's explore a few main avenues.

Most commonly, He speaks directly into our spirits. This will often come through our thoughts. It takes time to learn the difference between our thoughts, the devil's voice, and God's voice. We often sense the presence of the Holy Spirit when a prophetic word is brought or when we believe that God is speaking to us. But what we are hearing from God must always agree with the written Word of God. Appropriate the Word of God into your life so that you can rightly discern the voice of God when He speaks.

God at times speaks audibly. Hearing the actual voice of God is not as common; it is often dramatic, shocking, and amazing. I can count on one hand the number of times I have had these encounters. One such time I was in my living room seeking God, and suddenly, a loud voice filled the room. It freaked me out—I was completely caught off guard, but at the same time it felt natural. The voice carried the very familiar presence of God Himself. God told me something I urgently needed to be made aware of, which began a series of events that would forever change my life.

There are other ways that God speaks to us, such as visions, dreams, and heavenly visitations. His Spirit also leads us. For instance, we learn to become sensitive to the Holy Spirit's presence and His approval or disapproval of our actions and words. In other situations, it may be something seemingly simple but equally important, such as being sensitive to whether God's peace was present rather than a sense of striving and pressure.

Regularly hearing God's voice is a result of an intimate relationship with Him. I often find myself thinking about the statement Jesus said to His disciples, "Very truly I tell you, the Son can do nothing by himself; He can do only what He sees his Father doing, because whatever the Father does the Son also does" (John 5:19 NIV). This is a model for us as followers of Christ, especially for those who desire to move in the prophetic realm. Jesus told us how He lived life. He heard and saw His Father do everything first.

As I mentioned earlier, my story of hearing God's voice was birthed out of desperation. I simply was not going to go on without hearing Him. I grew up in a conservative church that didn't operate in many of the gifts of the Holy Spirit. There were few instances of people praying in tongues however I had never even heard a prophecy at that church until the age of twenty-one therefore I had little understanding of Biblical prophecy. What I did have was extremely vivid spiritual dreams that God was giving me. I didn't know that they were prophetic dreams or visions at that time. I only knew these were not normal. They were not nightmares but insights into another realm. At times, I looked into the future and would see what was to come. I would awake in the middle of the night singing songs to the Lord that I had never heard before.

These encounters captured my attention. God was communicating with me, but I had no reference point for it, as no one I knew had talked about such experiences.

What I did know during this same time was that I was surrounded by people who would do something based on the statement that "God had told them". I would watch these people carry out what they claimed God had said, and in many cases what they had claimed to be "God-directed", turned into terrible disasters, great losses and embarrassing or shameful situations. I became so aware and perturbed by these out-workings of "God-said" decisions that I developed almost a repulsion for this type of proclamation.

Once I became filled with Holy Spirit, however, I quickly became obsessed with wanting to learn to hear and discern the voice and leading of God. I was so hungry to hear God's voice in my daily life that I would not settle for anything else. I simply would not blindly trust "God-said" statements anymore; I wanted to take hold of God for myself and be 100 percent certain that what I heard was in fact His voice and not my imagination or emotions.

CONSISTENTLY HEARING GOD'S VOICE

Consistently hearing God's voice comes as a result of a few practices. Being born again is the most important requirement to hearing God's voice. We know that God speaks to the unsaved too, but I'm referring here to a consistent encountering of His voice. If you have surrendered your life to Jesus and He is the Lord of your life, then God will speak to you in a variety of ways. Even if we are unsaved or not walking with Him, God's heart is to pursue us and call us out of darkness and into His family.

I was repulsed by hypocrisy in the church and became completely backslidden and running from God. But during this time, I had one of the most radical encounters of my life. I was visited by two seven-foot angels in the night while I slept, and they took me in the spirit where I met with Jesus for several hours. This changed my life. As much as we want to define God, He is outside of our rules and definitions. His sheep know His voice. "They will never follow a stranger; in fact, they will run away from him because they do not recognize a stranger's voice" (John 10:5 NIV). Jesus, the Holy Spirit, and Father God will speak to people at various times in their unsaved state, calling them toward His goodness and mercy.

The truth is that God chooses to speak to His family. The prophetic gift can be in operation to a degree even without an intimate relationship with God, but the true prophtic gift requires the discernment and maturity of a seasoned believer. There was a sad occasion in my life in which a man I had known for a long time had become ensnared in perversion and adultery. I was genuinely attempting to help him because he was my friend, but he was twisted in his mind because of the sin he had fallen into. Amid this, he attempted on a couple of occasions, to speak "prophetic visions" to me. But the purity of his eye gate had been polluted and tarnished. I was aware of this and was guarded and wary of what he was saying. I went straight to God, and He clarified to me that this man was offering me something that was not from the Father's heart. It was so important for me to hear God's voice for myself during this time. Never trust everything you hear, but discern whether or not the "wells" of people's lives are safe to drink water from. I will verify with the Lord if what has been prophesied over me is accurate.

Never give up asking God questions, even it if feels like He has not responded to you in a while. Keep asking. God does not always respond right away. He can also send messengers to deliver His answer, which is frequently seen throughout the Bible. We also see that God responds in visions, heavenly visitations and dreams, which are manifestations of His voice and Spirit that are leading us into His will.

The Lord also speaks to us through His written Word. I cannot count how many times God has spoken to me directly from His Word as I have been reading my Bible. His Word is living and powerful it was written just for you in that moment. God still speaks, and we are to pursue His voice with passion and tenacity. Learn to interact with God in as many ways as possible. I love how at times I will hear His voice speaking gently, yet powerfully into my spirit and heart, and then He will confirm it later in other ways.

Become familiar with God's voice. Before we even discuss the prophetic applications, be sure that you are accurately hearing the Lord for your own life and journey. Be sure that when you step out in faith, you are following Him and not risking your future on vain imaginations. Become someone who pursues the heart of God as well as His voice.

When mentoring people, I look for those who don't just want to receive the anointing I carry, but for those who want a relationship with me. In the same way, when we pursue God's voice, we must not objectify God's voice, but value and honor the person He is. Our relationship with Him becomes a romance. We hear our lover's heart—not the instructions or commands of an employer. God is inviting us into His heart, where we hear His voice and rest secure in who we are in Him.

CHAPTER 3

GOD'S DREAM SHARED WITH YOU

If God opened up time and made it possible for you to observe how He made all of creation as recorded in the book of Genesis, you would want to take part in it, right? The amazing thing is that God is still at work, creating and breathing life today, and you're invited. Right now God is excited about all that He is doing, and He wants to share it with us. He wants to tell us what He is about to do, then have us watch in amazement as it unfolds.

He wants to share more than just His plans for us. He wants to talk about His feelings, His views and opinions; He wants to give us His insights and plans for other people as well. He wants to use us to bring others to His salvation, freedom and healing. God wants to tell us His plans to bring justice to injustice, and give us the keys and strategies for people, communities, and even nations so they can experience freedom. God wants to talk to us about anything He pleases. It will catch us off guard because God is an infinite being.

God does nothing in the earth unless He first reveals it to His servants the prophets. Amos said, "Surely the Sovereign LORD does nothing without revealing His plan to His servants the prophets" (Amos 3:7 NIV). The amazing part of this is that Jesus took that a step further and said that His sheep hear His voice (see John 10:27). This does not negate the need for prophets, for prophets will always be a unique and much-needed pillar in the body of Christ. But what it does mean is that no matter who you are, as a son or daughter of Father God, He wants to talk to you. You can learn to hear Him.

God is interested in sharing with us is not just to intrigue us, although it does that, but also to cause our faith to increase. We hear Him say what He is going to do, and then, watch Him do all He promised. Through that process, our faith becomes resolute and we can see through repeated testimonies that God proves that He is good and dependable.

The Scriptures tell us, "But without faith it is impossible to please Him, for he who comes to God must believe that He is, and that He is a rewarder of those who diligently seek Him" (Hebrews 11:6). God is looking for us to operate in faith, and that faith brings Him pleasure. Because God is so abundantly generous and wants to bless us, He becomes frustrated and even displeased when we doubt. Our lack of faith restricts Him from being able to pour out His affection and provision. When we believe God, and trust Him at His word, the channel between us stays open, allowing the delivery of the promises and supplies. God has a vested interest in growing our faith, but we need to do our part and believe.

Honoring what God chooses to reveal will cause greater measures of His goodness to be entrusted to us. As we are faithful with the little He has shown us, He releases even more. As we are proven trustworthy with what we have, we are then qualified to be given more. Understand that God's heart for our well-being is one of complete joy and generosity. Having a sound grasp on this helps us to see through His eyes, both when He speaks to us initially and throughout the entire process.

While my three sons are still toddlers, I simply cannot try to tell them all the dreams and plans I have for them. I cannot explain to them all my gained knowledge and wisdom, for how could they possibly be ready at the ages of three and under?

My family was planning a vacation overseas to New Zealand to spend time with our extended family. It would be obsurd of me to give my boys all the ticket and travel itinerary information. It would be too much for them. They don't have a grid for all those details. What I did was start telling my oldest that we were going to be getting on a big airplane all together and fly to New Zealand to see some of our family. Even though this was five months prior to the trip, his first reaction was, "Can we go now?". Little children don't have an understanding of time frames and advanced details so if want them have an understanding of the plans than you have to start simply.

Prior to our trip I took him to the local airport and I sat there with him, holding him on the side of the runway. We sat together and watched the different planes take off and land as it's one of his favorite things to do. This actual experience at an airport caused him to understand that people were inside of these planes. I simply explained to him that when it was our time to go we were going to get on one of those planes and fly to somewhere else to visit some of our family who he has only seen and talked to via video calls. Slowly, he started to get the message. Then he immediately asked me again if we were leaving now. I had to explain to him, "It's going to be in a little while."

My son is extremely intelligent, but I need to package information in a simple and small, bite-sized form so he gets the message and understands. He has trouble at times understanding why things don't always happen immediately, but he is learning. Again it's too much to begin to tell him what we are going to do every day while we are there. But when he gets there with us, it will all unfold in front of him, to his enjoyment.

This is just one example of how God slowly reveals things to us. We can easily misunderstand or assume specifics when He talks. God has everything planned, but all the details are too much for us right now. He will show us everything when we are ready. Right now, however, He is only releasing a "breadcrumb trail" that we can follow day by day. God is wise enough to only release small bits at a time so we are not overwhelmed or intimidated by the greatness of His plans.

The enormity of God's grand plan for us is so big that we are not ready for it, at least not ready for all of it. In Exodus 33:20, God said to Moses, "You cannot see My face; for no man shall see Me, and live." God is so great and awesome that simply looking at Him in physical form would be too overwhelming for us, even to the point of death. What God did, in His incredible wisdom, was to send His Son Jesus in human form, so that we could relate to what the Father is like. Jesus came to represent the Father in all His greatness, but in a measure we could handle. Any more and we would short circuit.

In the same way, if God revealed His amazing, excessively generous blueprint for us all at once, we would probably have a meltdown. It would be damaging if He did. The requirements, sacrifices, and personal costs would seem so overwhelming that most of us would refuse to go ahead with God's plan. It's important to understand this principle the next time you wonder why God hasn't shown you more details, explained Himself more clearly, or answered all your questions about your journey. Instead, from time to time, He gives us sneak peeks into the blueprints of His dreams. that are like breadcrumbs on our trail. They are little hints, clues, and messages that keep us walking in the direction of our destiny.

If God is calling you to do something or to go somewhere—for instance, move to a different part of the country or even emigrate to another country — He may not tell you all the specifics and details of where you are headed. He may only give you instructions that start you moving in the right direction. He understands that right now you may refuse to go to the place He is telling you because of the personal cost of the journey or the actual destination is not to your liking.

In His wisdom He will get you to start walking, moving, or thinking in a certain direction so that in time you will be ready for God to reveal more details as to what His purpose is for you in that particular field. For example, God said to Abram (his name was later changed by God to Abraham): "Go from your country, your people and your father's household to the land I will show you" (Genesis 12:1 NIV). The details were to come later. Doesn't this seem almost unfair?

In other words, God said, "Get up, leave your family home and land, and to go to this land I will show you. But I'm not telling you what or where that land is yet. You are going to trust Me and find out along the journey." Several generations later, Abram's descendants were still walking out the request, leaving four hundred years of slavery in Egypt to be led by Moses through the desert wilderness toward a Promised Land they were not quite sure of yet (see Exodus 14).

Like the children of Israel, your journey will require you to follow the cloud by day and the pillar of fire by night: "And the LORD went before them by day in a pillar of cloud to lead the way, and by night in a pillar of fire to give them light, so as to go by day and night" (Exodus 13:21). The grave mistake that the children of Israel made was that they began to murmur and complain in the process. They didn't understand God's dream, and so they walked through some extended discomfort (see Exodus 16:2). God was not pleased with their complaining and unbelief. Abraham began the journey and Joshua ended it when he led Abraham's descendants across the Jordan into the Promised Land of Canaan. Promise fulfilled, dream realized. Even though at times the Israelites went kicking and screaming toward the promise, God was and always will be true to His promises.

God shares His dreams with us so we have something to look toward and partner with. He shares His plans to breathe purpose and identity into us. We were designed to fulfill our purpose and destiny, but we must choose to cooperate with God and choose His way. We can see the purity and vulnerability of God's nature in the Garden of Eden in that He did not seek to control Adam and Eve relationally. He gave them free will. He placed one forbidden tree in the garden so that they could exercise that freedom. If they chose to disobey and eat the fruit, all of humanity would be infected with the deadliest virus—sin.

God put the Tree of the Knowledge of Good and Evil in the Garden and told Adam and Eve, "Of every tree of the garden you may freely eat; but of the tree of the knowledge of good and evil you shall not eat, for in the day that you eat of it you shall surely die" (Genesis 2:16–17). That death was a spiritual death, but ultimately it was a physical death, too. Adam and Eve disobeyed, and as a result the whole world has been damaged by sin. God was amazing in that He shared His ideal and left it to Adam and Eve to choose. We can also see this same nature in Jesus Christ.

God told the Israelites on several occasions that He set before them life and death, but it was their choice. For example, on one occasion, God said, "I call heaven and earth as witnesses today against you, that I have set before you life and death, blessing and cursing; therefore choose life, that both you and your descendants may live" (Deuteronomy 30:19). God values our free will so much that He will not interfere with it—to the point that people are choosing every day to go to an eternity without God, and even God won't stop them. He will send His children angelic visitations and dreams to plead with them to accept Jesus, but He will never force anyone.

God has a dream for each of us. Just like God did in the garden with Adam and Eve, that dream is an offer but it is not forced. He reveals sneak peeks, messages, and promises into our hearts so we can freely choose to fulfill His plans and dreams for our lives. That's why the Bible says in Matthew 22:14, "For many are invited, but few are chosen" (NIV). Hearing God's dream is equally as important as God's dream itself. Responding in agreement and moving toward the dream, whether we fully understand the big picture, or if it's uncomfortable or inconvenient, is essential to the dream coming to pass.

God's dreams are intimate and precious. He watches the way we treat them and the value we apply to what He shares with us. In some ways He tests us to see if we will be good stewards of what He allows us to know. If we are found trustworthy, He will entrust us with more.

The exciting adventure of your life begins and is fulfilled with the acceptance of God's dream over you. You are invited to look into marvelous mysteries so that you can see the magnitude of God promises, but you must say "yes" to Him. It is at this point that your journey truly begins. From there you need to continue saying "yes" right up till the point that all that He has said is fulfilled.

Once we learn to become good stewards of this on a personal level, God will begin to expand our sphere of influence to others, and from there to groups, communities, cities, nations, continents, and even to the world. One thing we always must remember is that God dreams big and wants you along for the ride.

ENTERING YOUR PROMISED LAND

Look at Canaan, the land of promise, God's inheritance for the children of Israel who were Abraham's descendants. The land was occupied by strong people with fortified cities like Jericho (see Joshua 6). The children of Israel were ex-slaves with little military background or any grid for land ownership. God walked them into the land step by step; along the way He gave them instructions that sometimes didn't make any sense.

For example, in conquering Jericho, they were instructed to walk around the city for seven days, and then on the seventh day they were to walk around the city seven times and blow trumpets. That is not a smart invasion strategy by human wisdom, but it was to God. On the last day when they shouted and blew the trumpets, God supernaturally caused all the fortified city walls to crumble and fall. Because they obeyed, God acted. When the walls fell, it was time for them to run inside the city and overtake it.

When it comes to inheriting promises, the entitlement mentality says, "Jesus did it all for me, I don't need to do anything except receive." This mentality is not God's model, however. God promised Abraham a land He would give to him; He showed Moses the land He was giving to the Israelites. But it took sacrifice and obedience—

all harnessed with God-breathed wisdom to fulfill these promises. The same is still true in our lives today. I am not suggesting that we strive in our own strength and work for the blessing of God. There is a grace and rest, yet at the same time our faith is confirmed by our actions and works, not just by our words.

Some of what God speaks happens instantly and creates a paradigm shift in our lives. But when it comes to destiny and inheritance-type prophetic words, visions or promises, there will almost always be a trail of obedience involving personal cost, wisdom, and endurance. We need to be changed, trained and qualified before we can realize our promised destiny. What an amazing thing that we are invited to preview God's plans for our lives! He is showing His created sons and daughters such high esteem and honor, by granting us the privilege of knowing His intentions and blueprints for the earth. What generosity and extravagant trust that God would reveal His secrets to us!

CHAPTER 4

GIDEON'S WISDOM: VERIFYING WHAT YOU HAVE HEARD

You have now heard from God...or have you? Your answer could be your worst mistake. What if what you thought was God's voice was only your imagination? What if you wanted God to say something so badly that you talked yourself into believing that He said it? What if you are about to take a risk on that very message and regret it for the rest of your life? What if God has spoken to you, and His words have shaken you to the core and you are too afraid to do what He asked? Or what if God's words don't make sense to you? I have learned to confirm what I sense God is saying.

The Scriptures tell us in Proverbs 29:20, "Do you see a man hasty in his words? There is more hope for a fool than for him." It is much wiser to confirm what you think God said, is what He, in fact, did say. Our emotions, ambitions, and fears can be so deceiving that we cannot simply trust every thought that floats through our consciousness. Even if the most reputable prophet in your life speaks a word over you that they claim is from the Lord, it is your responsibility to verify that what was declared was indeed God's voice.

Why do we need to test the prophetic? Many of us are hungry, even desperate to hear God speak. We long to hear a word regarding our spouse, our children, finances, employment, ministry and callings, which are all good things, right? The problem comes when *we* decide what God should say or do. This happens simply because of a lack of knowing how God operates.

The problem, especially for those younger in their journey with God, is that their excitement, and unharnessed zeal can sometimes actually become a hindrance. Zeal is such a powerful attribute, but Proverbs 19:2 tells us that "desire [zeal or enthusiasm] without knowledge [wisdom] is not good—how much more will hasty feet miss the way!" (NIV). What that means is that having an abundance of energy and enthusiasm with an absence of wisdom and common sense will result in embarrassing and shameful outcomes.

The reason I am focusing on this principle specifically is that when we are zealous and desperate to hear God, we actually have the ability to fabricate a message from Him. We can become gullible and receive a word from others too hastily. If we are impatient, we can latch on to a prophetic vision and run with it before we have stopped to confirm with God that what we have heard or been told has come from Him and is not merely our imagination.

THE EXAMPLE OF GIDEON

I highly respect Gideon. In Judges 6:11-40 he was a hero who became renown by saving Israel when he conquered the invading and pillaging army. But he did not start out that way. According to the Biblical account, he began threshing wheat and hiding from the enemy in a wine press. Judges 6:11–12 picks it up there:

> Now the Angel of the LORD came and sat under the terebinth tree which was in Ophrah, which belonged to Joash the Abiezrite, while his son Gideon threshed wheat in the winepress, in order to hide it from the Midianites. And the Angel of the LORD appeared to him, and said to him, 'The LORD is with you, you mighty man of valor!'

The angel of the Lord appeared to Gideon when he was hiding in what appears to be a beaten-down, defeatist mentality. When this passage refers to the Angel of the Lord, it is referring to the Lord Himself appearing. We can see this confirmed later in verse 14, where the "Angel of the Lord" means "Angel of Yahweh." Some interpret the Hebrew to mean, Yahweh or God Himself.

The Angel of the Lord's opening address to Gideon was, "The LORD is with you, you mighty man of valor!" (Judges 6:12). Look at Gideon's immediate response found in verse 13: "O my lord, if the LORD is with us, why then has all this happened to us? And where are all His miracles, which our fathers told us about, saying, 'Did not the LORD bring us up from Egypt?' But now the LORD has forsaken us and delivered us into the hands of the Midianites."

Although Gideon was struggling along with the people as they were heavily oppressed by the enemy, the angel of the Lord appeared right in front of him. And even though many would see Gideon as cowardly, God called him and identified him in light of his destiny: "The LORD is with you, you mighty man of valor!" All this was said to a man hiding in a wine press. No sooner had the angel finished that statement that Gideon responded negatively with doubt, unbelief, and complaints.

The Lord ignored Gideon's whining and reiterated, "Go in this might of yours, and you shall save Israel from the hand of the Midianites. Have I not sent you?" (Judges 6:14). I love how God ignores our temporary unbelief and still calls to us to be a part of His grand design. We cannot stay in doubt if we want to ever inherit His promises. Gideon says in verse 15, "O my Lord, how can I save Israel? Indeed my clan is the weakest in Manasseh, and I am the least in my father's house." Listen to God's encouraging response in verse 16: "And the LORD said to him, 'Surely I will be with you, and you shall defeat the Midianites as one man.'" Think of it! All this dialogue took place while God was standing right in front of Gideon.

Gideon asked for a sign in his offering of a young goat, some unleavened bread, and flour. He brought them all back to the Lord, who stood waiting for him. The Lord instructed Him to put these on a rock and pour the broth from the meat over all of it. Once Gideon did that, the Lord touched the meat and the unleavened bread with His staff, and it was consumed in fire. Then the Angel of the Lord departed from his sight. Gideon suddenly realized that it was truly God who had been speaking all this to Him (see Judges 6:17–24).

Many believers categorize Gideon as a coward and a doubter. Agreed, Gideon had some faith and identity issues, but he was no fool. If this was truly God, there is no question about Gideon's willingness to be obedient to Him. In fact, Gideon wanted absolute assurance that everything he was hearing was without a doubt, God's voice.

God had Gideon take a bull for a burnt offering, and pull down the wooden idol of Baal, a pagan demon god. God was preparing Gideon for the next task, which was Gideon's destiny. If we look at this prophetically, we see that God had Gideon destroy the very thing the enemy was using for his purposes, which would then release the full blessing of the Lord over that territory. God used Gideon as a spearhead to bring freedom to the people. Once Gideon had finished this assignment, avoided being killed by the demon god worshippers, he was positioned and ready.

Then we see what I refer to as the wisdom of Gideon. Gideon called out to God in the rest of Judges 6, asking for more confirmation for the greater task ahead—the saving of the nation of Israel.

> So Gideon said to God, 'If You will save Israel by my hand as You have said—look, I shall put a fleece of wool on the threshing floor; if there is dew on the fleece only, and it is dry on all the ground, then I shall know that You will save Israel by my hand, as You have said.' And it was so. When he rose early the next morning and squeezed the fleece together, he wrung the dew out of the fleece, a bowlful of water. Then Gideon said to God, 'Do not be angry with me, but let me speak just once more: Let me test, I pray, just once

more with the fleece; let it now be dry only on the fleece,
but on all the ground let there be dew.' And God did so that
night. It was dry on the fleece only, but there was dew on all
the ground (Judges 6:36–40).

In all our teachings, books, conferences, worship albums, and great church sermons, how is it that we have slipped away from this level of tenacity to search out God's will for each of our lives? If you do anything in your pursuit of God as a son or daughter of the King, once you are sure you are hearing His voice, then build a habit of confirming it.

WHAT QUESTIONS ARE YOU ASKING?

The issue perhaps isn't that you're not asking God a question, but that you are asking the wrong question. James reminds us, "You ask and do not receive, because you ask amiss, that you may spend it on your pleasures" (James 4:3). He means that his readers have not received answers to their prayers because of their own agendas and intentions.

Do you remember as a child asking loaded questions that could only be answered certain ways? For instance, "Mommy, I want that toy, nothing else will make me happy. Can I have it?" We learn the art of emotional manipulation from an early age and then think nothing of implementing the same strategy with God when we are older. Twisting His hand, or so we think, to get what we want, is not the way it works. That is not asking God His will; rather, that is dictating your will to God and asking Him to agree with you.

This looks like Aaron the high priest building a golden calf for the children of Israel in the desert, and then asking God to bless them in spite of their lust and idolatry. (see Exodus 32). This is not a pleasant truth, but a needed truth all the same.

There is a huge difference between asking God for something you have already set your heart on, and asking God to reveal His will and plan for your life without a predetermined agenda. True submission to the King of heaven; says this: "Your kingdom come, Your will be done, on earth as it is in heaven" (Matthew 6:10 NIV). "Asking amiss" (James 4:2-3) is deciding something and asking God to bless what you have already decided, when more than likely it is not His will.

WHAT OUTCOME DO YOU WANT?

That leads us to Romans 12:2, where Paul writes, "And do not be conformed to this world, but be transformed by the renewing of your mind, that you may prove what is that good and acceptable and perfect will of God." It's important here to understand that "good" and "acceptable" are different from "perfect." The promised outcome should always influence our motives and actions, so let's look a little closer at the three outcomes offered in this scripture.

THE ACCEPTABLE OUTCOME

The acceptable outcome is when God accepts your decision, but it's not really a part of His plan for your life. What you chose was not necessarily evil per se, but it was not what God intended for you in His plan. Paul wrote, "'I have the right to do anything,' you say—but not everything is beneficial." (1 Corinthians 6:12 NIV).

God, in His grace and care for your life, is going to bless you and draw you to Himself with His goodness. For example, when Adam and Eve chose to disobey God and eat the forbidden fruit in the garden, God could have killed them on the spot, but in His goodness, He made a way that was acceptable for them to move forward. Instead of God killing Adam and Eve, He killed animals to cover their nakedness before He cast them out of the garden. God went to the extent of making skins for them to cover their nakedness—His goodness made a way of escape and provision even when Adam and Eve chose the wrong path.

Please understand that I am not condoning sin here in any way. Rather, I am outlining that when you choose to sin or pursue something that isn't God's best all the while asking God to bless you, He will still make a way for you and protect you. However, you will miss out on the *very best* God has for your life. When we attempt to get God to accept our choice, we are settling for something less than we were made for—selling our birthright to God's best where the real treasure is. We must desire more than the acceptable outcome.

THE GOOD OUTCOME

The good outcome is usually a result of *some* of what God has said and a *little* of what we wanted. This again is similar to the acceptable outcome as it is less than perfect and it is missing out on the best. The good outcome is usually closer to getting it right than the previous scenario. It may look like you are hearing God accurately but being hasty and not waiting on His timing; instead of waiting, you're just jumping ahead into something prematurely.

The good outcome will make you happy and feel measures of blessing because it is good, but it will always fall short of the best. Good outcomes are many times mistaken for the perfect will of God for an individual's life. But why settle for good when you can have perfect goodness planned by a God who only dreams the best for His children?

THE PERFECT OUTCOME

The perfect outcome has come from perfect obedience and submission to exactly what God spoke. It is a result of your inquiring of the Lord and doing exactly what He showed you in the timing and outworking of what He revealed. With every purpose, there is time and judgment (see Ecclesiastes 8:6). Godly maturity will not just discern what God is showing, but also reveal insight into God's timing. It's not that God will always give exact time frames, but wisdom does not jump ahead of Him.

Not only do you verify what God showed you, but also you discern His instructions on the timing. And it's worth it. It's worth every aspect of all that will be required of you to see the promise come to pass. Living in the perfect will of God looks different than living in the good or acceptable will of God.

Having clarified that, not everything will end up perfect on its own; it takes an ear to hear God's voice, a heart to let Him lead us into His will, a setting aside of our agenda, as well as the grace of wisdom and patience to do it God's way. No amount of desperation and anxiety is worth ending up with something less than God's best for you.

The Bible enlightens us with a crucial key when it says, "It is the glory of God to conceal a matter; but the glory of kings is to search out a matter" (Proverbs 25:2). God doesn't cheaply post instruction signs on our personal journeys in easy-to-find locations. He conceals them. And we, as His heirs, His sons and daughters, kings and queens, are now honored with the privilege of seeking them out.

The Scriptures tells us again: "The secret of the LORD is with those who fear Him, and He will show them His covenant" (Psalm 25:14). The word *fear* does not mean terror, but rather reverential respect for the Lord. Wisdom will instruct us to pursue God's voice through intimacy, a deep respect and honor of who He is. Like Gideon, when you think you have heard His voice, slow down and verify that you have heard correctly. It isn't being doubtful when you verify and check; it's wisdom. Once you are sure, follow God's instructions exactly as He has said without compromise. It may cost you, but it will be worth it. In my experience, there's always a price with the genuine will of God. Without cost, there is no value. It's not a matter of striving; it's pressing on toward the mark of your high call and the promises that God has laid out in front of you.

Many Christians have a mentality that if God said it, then they can have it. This is both right and wrong. It's right in that if God has spoken it to you, then it's your inheritance. It's wrong, however, in believing that His promises are unconditional. There are always requirements to fulfill and wisdom necessary to walk out God's promises. This is where many people leave the pathway. It takes faith, obedience, and God's counsel and wisdom to inherit your promise.

CHAPTER 5

GUARDING YOUR HEART IN THE PROCESS

GUARD YOUR HEART

The writer of Proverbs admonishes us, "Above all else, guard your heart, for everything you do flows from it" (Proverbs 4:23 NIV). If your heart becomes toxic with offense, doubt, unbelief or unforgiveness, it is guaranteed to show up in the external expression of your life. If these conditions are present within your heart, they will affect the other facets of your life as well. They can take you off course and cause you to miss your destination. This is why Proverbs 4:23 uses the language "above all else," or to put it another way, "most importantly." We must guard our hearts, for our outcomes and destinies are at stake.

You heard God speak, you became excited about the promise, you checked and confirmed that it was God who was speaking, and then you agreed with Him and accepted the offer of His promise. Even though you hold the destiny in your heart, life has been happening and the trail has been hard. The environment and circumstances have been against you, and at times, much like Gideon, it's frustrating wondering where God is and how His plan could ever come to pass in your life. Sound familiar? Here are a few key areas where we must guard our hearts as we walk out the promises God has given to us.

EXTENDED DELAY

At times there are seasons of extended delay, where we are waiting on the promises of God to come to pass. We may question whether we heard God in the first place. The fact is that God's timing is always perfect. However, often that timing feels late by our expectations. These are the seasons that are so important for us to sit quietly in patient faith, waiting on the promises of God. We trust that God's timing is always best, and trust Him to work everything out.

Some delays are self-imposed through disobedience or unbelief in what God is requiring of us, and they can be challenging to walk through. The key to remember when we have sabotaged what God has asked of us, is that if we repent and get it right with Him, then "God works for the good of those who love him, who have been called according to his purpose" (Romans 8:28 NIV). It may take some time. Remember, God promises are always on offer, even if we get them wrong. God may need to change circumstances to work them out; it may look differently than we originally thought. But God will work it out. He is in control, not us. *Guard your heart in the process.*

OPPOSING CIRCUMSTANCES

In the beginning of the book of Genesis when God began creating the world, He did not start with a perfect scenario. The Scriptures tell us that in the beginning the earth was without form and void; it was covered in darkness, far from what God was about to create. Then God spoke. When God speaks creative destiny, it is often into situations and circumstances that are completely the opposite of what He is calling forth in us, like calling light out of darkness. Life can suddenly take a turn in the opposite direction, creating situations and scenarios that make what God said seem impossible. If God declares a thing, like in Genesis 1, then it's going to happen. The circumstances that create obstacles and impossibilities, only make the promises more apparent so that only God gets all the credit and glory. *Again, guard your heart in the process.*

THE ENEMY SPEAKING AGAINST GOD'S GOODNESS

We must always be aware of the enemy's strategies and plans. The devil wants to steal, kill, and destroy God's plan for our lives (see John 10:10). But we must remember that he has absolutely no power over us except that which we give him, just like it was in the garden between Eve and the serpent (see Genesis 3). The serpent had no power over Eve; he only used suggestive statements that planted a seed of doubt toward God. It was Eve who decided. The weapon that the serpent, the devil, used was the doubt of God's goodness toward Adam and Eve. He questioned if God was in fact wanting the best for them or holding them back. The same ploys are being used today against us.

We must guard our minds from the lies of the enemy. Jesus referred to Satan as "a murderer from the beginning, and [who] does not stand in the truth, because there is no truth in him. When he speaks a lie, he speaks from his own resources, for he is a liar and the father of it" (John 8:44). Satan is also referred to as "the accuser of the brethren" (Romans 12:10), which means he is like a prosecuting lawyer in court, pointing out our sins and shortfalls before God. But he is also the accuser of God. Beware of the enemy trying to build a court case in your mind against the goodness and faithfulness of God. *Above all else, guard your heart.*

THE DOUBT AND UNBELIEF OF OTHERS

Be careful who you share your dreams with, because doubters and haters can crush dreams. This is wise business advice I received as a young man, which is just as applicable in the realm of the prophetic. Not everyone is as excited for you as you may be for them. Even well meaning people, such as close family members and friends, may not yet walk in the level of faith required to inherit the promise you currently hold onto. They may have had experiences in which they put things in the "too hard" basket and gave up on their dream; they think they are doing you a favor and protecting you from getting your hopes dashed like they did. You must protect your God dreams from the naysayers and doubters, or they'll have a chance to plant doubt and despair in your mind in an attempt to cause you to question if God is going to come through for you. *Guard your heart in the process.*

GUARDING YOUR HEART

Guarding your heart in the process of walking out any promised word or vision, especially when it pertains to an emotive area (i.e., a future spouse, finances, pregnancies, and children), is so essential to arriving at your destination. When I refer to guarding your heart, that really doesn't mean "not getting your hopes up." No, God wants your hopes up—that is what we call faith. Faith is the vehicle that pulls your promise nearer. Rather, it is being on guard so external circumstances, opposition, or the enemy's lies cannot steal your hope and cause you to question what God said to you.

It's important that you walk with wisdom in this area while still maintaining your eager anticipation. Don't become skeptical; have a balanced guard over your heart in walking out the process of your prophetic promise. It is healthy to receive a word and "shelf it," because with some words it is hard to tell if they are God-breathed or not. When we receive a word, is it necessary to check with God to be certain it is, in fact, His word and nothing else.

At times, especially if it's an emotive word, it can be incredibly difficult to decipher whether you are hearing from God or someone's emotional imitation of "the word of the Lord." In all situations I show grace and I will go and pray about "the word of the Lord". I don't want to discourage people from stepping out and believing the Holy Spirit for the prophetic. I will always teach people how to examine a word before they deliver it. I pray over the specific words and consider it from time to time, but I do not allow that word to direct or influence my decision-making until I know it's from God!

Above all else, guard your heart, for from it flow the issues of life. Offense, disappointment, and despair are all emotions that can damage the state of our hearts, particularly toward God's goodness and provision.

You have two enemies: the devil and your own unhealed emotions. The devil will always try to get you to believe that God has abandoned you and is not for you, or that you are on your own and all is lost. However, your own emotions will do great damage by sabotaging God's best for your life if they are not controlled and submitted to God's will. Paul reminds us, "For the flesh lusts against the Spirit, and the Spirit against the flesh; and these are contrary to one another, so that you do not do the things that you wish" (Galatians 5:17).

GOD'S FORMULA FOR PROPHETIC ENDURANCE

God told Habakkuk to "Write down the revelation and make it plain on tablets so that a herald may run with it" (Habakkuk 2:2 NIV). This is God's formula for prophetic endurance. And endurance is a key to guarding your heart as a promise is in the process. The moment you hear from God, wake up from a prophetic dream, or someone delivers a prophetic word to you, excitement wells up inside. But the passing of time and the busyness of life can cause these words and visions to be forgotten or even abandoned.

Writing words down in a journal or safe place and regularly revisiting these promises and dreams God has shown you will keep the words fresh in your heart. This is an encouraging and life-giving habit to form in your routines, reminding you each time you go back to read these that God's plan is specific and unique, that they are good and filled with hope (see Jeremiah 29:11). Then you, the runner, are sent out to journey the coming days, weeks, or years with this written promise.

Do not grow weary, despondent, or discouraged when God's promises do not come to pass right away. This seems to be a trait in the realm of the prophetic. For when it does not come to pass in the time frame you expected, do not give up on it, because it will come at God's perfect and preordered time and will not delay. But keeping your heart right throughout this process is imperative to seeing what God has promised come to pass.

There have been a few words I knew God had spoken to me about in the past where my heart doubted and despaired—we have all reacted that way. Just like the children of Israel who murmured in the wilderness and wandered in their hearts, God's promises can pass us by. A grateful, faith-filled heart will expedite your promise. An ungrateful heart, full of doubt, will delay it or even cause you to miss the promise. Keeping your heart right throughout the process will ensure you see Gods promises fulfilled.

There will be times where God will allow you to walk through a testing time. This is another trait I've grown to know in God's process, where we may be challenged either circumstantially or emotionally. This is a refining process, but also a qualifying one. For instance, in the natural, to get a promotion at work, you must pass certain unannounced tests from the employer—certain things that may stretch and grow you beyond your current capacity. Looking back over my walk with God, nothing has grown me more than times of adversity. It's not that God is causing the hardship, but He is using certain circumstances to test us, strengthening our endurance so we can come out on the other side ready and qualified for our new season, breakthrough, or promotion.

Psalm 75:6 says, "No one from the east or the west or from the desert can exalt themselves" (NIV). Therefore, we want to be mindful that certain adversities and challenges in life may be more than they appear; they may be the precursor to the fulfillment of the promise we are clinging to as we walk humbly before the

Lord. Keeping a right heart throughout the process requires an important ingredient: intense focus.

The writer of Hebrews tells us that we are to fix "our eyes on Jesus, the pioneer and perfecter of faith. For the joy set before him he endured the cross, scorning its shame, and sat down at the right hand of the throne of God" (Hebrews 12:2 NIV). The Son of God who was going through the most challenging trial and test of faith ever imaginable. We see Jesus holding fast and committing all He had and was to a prophetic promise of "the joy [glory] set before Him," which was victory, the redemption of humankind, and being seated at the right hand of the Father. James tells us:

> *My brethren, count it all joy when you fall into various trials, knowing that the testing of your faith produces patience. But let patience have its perfect work, that you may be perfect and complete, lacking nothing. If any of you lacks wisdom, let him ask of God, who gives to all liberally and without reproach, and it will be given to him. But let him ask in faith, with no doubting, for he who doubts is like a wave of the sea driven and tossed by the wind. For let not that man suppose that he will receive anything from the Lord; he is a double-minded man, unstable in all his ways (James 1:2–8).*

If we do not keep our hearts right through these processes, then we may be tempted to listen to the accusing voice of the enemy who subtly whispers words attempting to discredit God's faithfulness and goodness. If we consider these proposals from the enemy, our hearts darken and grow hard. If this happens, we play ourselves right into the devil's trap, and in some cases can disqualify ourselves from the blessing of breakthrough. Hebrews 3:8 tells us, "Therefore, as the Holy Spirit says, 'Today, if you hear His voice, do not harden your hearts as you did in the rebellion...'" Always remember that God does not tempt you; the devil does that. But God will test you and give you the grace to endure and pass the test!

The number one battle you will face in your emotions is the thought that God's promises are never going to come to pass. If you start to believe this, you have put yourself in grave danger. While faith is powerful because it draws God's blessings closer, fear is the antithesis of faith— powerful but destructive. I knew a person who would always speak negatively about certain areas of his life. He was desperate for what God had promised, but a seed of doubt, unbelief, and fear had sprung up in his heart. He would declare that his promises would never ever come to pass, and those promises were never fulfilled. What comes out of your mouth is what you will have in your life. Proverbs 18:21 states, "The tongue has the power of life and death, and those who love it will eat its fruit" (NIV). You are constantly sowing your future with your mouth. Choose your words wisely.

In most cases, God's promises *seem* impossible, they *feel* impossible. This is because God wants to grow you—to stretch the boundaries of your faith. When things seem impossible and you are tempted to become discouraged and despairing, do the opposite. Don't internalize your emotions; rather, allow faith to rise (even if it's forced at first), because faith is a decision, not a feeling.

Many Christians die in their own wilderness and don't see their Promised Land because of self-pity. They live out of their feelings instead of ruling from their spirits. Choose to make the decision to stay in faith and live above your emotions, speaking life to your future, no matter what stands in your way, no matter how many mountains you have to climb. If God said you can, that settles the debate.

Move forward and believe God. There is no passivity in the kingdom of heaven. This is an aggressive advance. Obtaining the promises of God is not for the faint of heart; you are going to have to discipline yourself to go the distance, and resolve within your heart to never negotiate or settle for anything less. If you are to receive God's promises in your life, then you are going to have to learn how to guard your heart in the process.

CHAPTER 6

HOLDING ON TO THE PROMISE OVER TIME

King David once said, "I would have lost heart, unless I had believed that I would see the goodness of the LORD in the land of the living" (Psalm 27:13). At various times during his life, David was in seasons of long and delayed hope. He endured incredible adversity that could have jeopardized his future. David was stating here that he would have given up on the promises if he had not decidedly held onto the hope that God's goodness would play out in his life.

We are talking about a young boy who was called out of the field while tending sheep and anointed by Samuel to be king of Israel (see 1 Samuel 16). This is the boy who slayed a giant named Goliath (see 1 Samuel 17), saved a king and a nation in one day, gained favor and ended up in the king's court. He was then persecuted and hunted by King Saul for a considerable portion of his life (see 1 Samuel 19). Yet David walked with God and in the process was changed, prepared and qualified to be the king he was anointed to be. It took time and though many difficulties suggested that what God said was impossible, it did come to pass.

What you believe matters. You must hold the promise in your heart and not lose focus or faith. If you will do this, then you will see the goodness of God played out in your life. What you decide and commit to believe is essential if you are going to inherit God's promises. Every child of God receives words of hope, some divinely spoken straight from the voice of God in personal relationship, some through prophetic words delivered via other people, and some through promises in God's written Word, the Bible. Many lose heart in the process and the promises never seem to arrive. These folks end up disillusioned and frustrated, thinking they have been forgotten by God. They have not been forgotten; they only need to remember to hold fast and cling to His promises. The Bible declares:

> *"God is not a man, so he does not lie.*
>
> *He is not human, so he does not change his mind.*
>
> *Has he ever spoken and failed to act?*
>
> *Has he ever promised and not carried it through?" (Numbers 23:19 NLT).*

Not everyone who starts the race holding onto a promise finishes—I wish it was easier. But every good thing that God promises requires our faith and endurance from the moment the promise is made until it is delivered. Faith, endurance, dedication, and much prayer are all ingredients needed to get to the destination without fainting along the way. Faith in God's promises despite all odds and the circumstances raging against us, is the key to inheriting promises. Only believe and you will see the goodness of God in the land of the living.

Holding onto your promise will ensure you inherit the promise. In Hebrews 11, we read about those God describes as heroes of the faith, or to put it differently, those who held to promises even though their circumstances seemed completely impossible. All these men and women believed God despite these opposing obstacles over long periods of time, some of them for their entire lifetimes. As a result, God was pleased with them.

Let's paint a picture to define what this looks like. In a royal monarchy, there is a king or queen who rules a nation or an empire. The king or queen who is crowned and seated on the throne over a kingdom will have a son or daughter who is more than offspring; that child is an heir to their throne. When the ruling king or queen steps down from the throne to retire, or passes away, the heir will be crowned the new king or queen. The heir is promised the throne and the crown, and will rule over the entire kingdom, because it is his or her birthright. However, that heir has to walk worthy of the throne all the way up to the point of being crowned. The heir cannot do anything that would disqualify him or her from the throne during the waiting process.

Consider the British royal family. Queen Elizabeth currently sits on the throne of England because her uncle, abdicated his birthright. The action put Queen Elizabeth in the direct line of succession to the throne. He pursued a woman outside of monarchy protocols, and because he was unwilling to comply with protocols, they were at an impasse. Ultimately he made his decision and forfeit the throne of England. He chose to abdicate his inheritance to obtain something that did not belong to him. This compromise was not befitting for a crowned king. As a result, he would never sit on the throne he was born to possess—he forfeited that honor.

The reason I have gone into such detail about this story about the British monarch is that a promise given to you is like a throne to which you are an heir. The way you walk is a direct reflection of what you believe. Believing the various promises will empower you to walk worthy of them. Trusting God and walking worthy of the promise will keep you from actions and compromises, which could cause you to miss out on the promise God has given.

It's important we grasp the concept that God is not in a rush to deliver promises to us; He is totally in control, calm, and always on time. It is us who often become distressed over promises not happening the way we would like them to. God is more interested in how we walk than in how long the journey takes. Let's take a step back, let go of the tendency to panic and learn to walk in real faith that trusts and believes that God is ordering our steps and empowering us for the journey.

A troublesome trait of the prophetic is that when God speaks or reveals a promise, the prophet or prophetic person will likely see it as a "now" reality, which may instead be a long way off in God's actuality. The prophet, who sees and hears into the future, often has the perception that what they are looking into is much closer than it is. The prophetic person is actually looking through the eyes of faith—seeing what is far off as though it is going to happen tomorrow. We get a better understanding of this by looking closer at Hebrews 11:1, which says that faith is "evidence of things not yet seen." Real faith sees now what is not yet seen in the natural.

This is where a young prophet who has not grasped this reality will undoubtedly encounter frustrations, not just for himself but also for those to whom he prophesies, if he promises unrealistic time frames. As I have previously mentioned, we must learn to discern both timing and judgment of a matter. There are two elements to consider here: the promissory message and God's timing.

It takes maturity to be able to be discerning and wise in this area. For instance, if you believe that a promise God has given you is going to take place in two years, but God's plans are a much longer time frame, then you will feel like giving up after the first two years. You set yourself up for disappointment. How do you run with endurance without losing your faith? How do you hold onto your promise and believe God against all odds, no matter how long it takes?

Proverbs 9:12 tells us, "If you are wise, your wisdom will reward you..." (NIV). In other words, making good decisions benefits you. Make a decision now to be determined to enter every promise that God has given you. You must sever ties with compromise, self-pity, self-comfort, discouragement, and despair. Quit comparing your journey to others' journeys, or predicting when God is going to do what He promises unless He has clearly, specifically, and undoubtedly told you the timing.

You must become dead to every other voice but God's, and only speak His language, the language of faith, as you navigate toward a destination you have likely never been to before. Respectfully shut out all other voices like doubt, criticism and unbelief, for they do not contribute to your future. Be content to wait patiently, and at the same time aggressively pursue God, with no ultimatum on His timing. True faith doesn't have exit clauses.

How bad do you want the promise? Is it casual or is it your inheritance—are you an heir or an abdicator? God believes you are an heir, which is what He calls you; you only need to make up your mind never to do anything that would compromise your walk toward the promise. You will discover that most get-rich-quick schemes are scams and that there is no such thing as easy money. Income and returns on investments take time, which is what makes them so valuable—if they came easily, there would be no real worth. The prophetic is the same: from the moment it is spoken until the time it is realized takes time, with a small percentage of exceptions in which God fast-tracks the delivery.

When I was brand new to the things of the Spirit of God, I was being mentored by a kind man I worked for at the time. He would invite me to come and eat at his house every few weeks. He would share wise principles and his own experiences with me. This was of great benefit to me. He would occasionally have a prophetic word for me that God had spoken to him privately as he would pray for me during the week. On one occasion, he delivered this word from the Lord to me: "My son, I am pleased with you, for you are growing and will continue to grow in my Spirit and Son. You will meet your wife."

That was it for this twenty-two-year-old young man. From the minute I left his home, I was practically asking God if each pretty girl I walked past was my wife—I was so excited and hyped up about it. The days turned into weeks, the weeks turned into months, my zeal and enthusiasm turned into despair and I was hurt. I had the word of the Lord, but in my inexperience, I did not understand God's timing on the fulfillment of His promises. Peter reminds us, "The Lord is not slow in keeping his promise, as some understand slowness. Instead he is patient with you, not wanting anyone to perish, but everyone to come to repentance" (2 Peter 3:9 NIV).

It wasn't until almost a decade later that I waited at the front of a church with tears shamelessly rolling down my face as my beautiful bride walked down the aisle of the church we were married in. God was faithful and never lied to me. It just wasn't in the time frame I initially thought. When it seems God is slow in delivering the promise we are so impatiently waiting for, it is usually for our benefit. If I had married my wife years earlier, I would have likely hurt her as I wasn't ready to steward her heart. My singleness and occasional loneliness, along with my youthful pride and ego, would have said I was ready, but I wasn't. It took the hand of God shaping me and training me along the journey through some difficult seasons to shave off the rough edges of my personality and character so I would be qualified for the promise and wouldn't damage the treasure. God is not holding back the best; you simply may not be ready for it as you're still in the training, shaping, and qualifying process.

God's "soon" and our "soon" are two very different definitions. Our soon may be shaped by our own desperation, hastiness, loneliness, despair or depression, which are unstable. God's soon, on the other hand, can be understood by looking at His wisdom.

I am so encouraged when I look at Jesus's purity , integrity and courage of His heart to trust the Father in His own journey. Jesus is "the author and finisher of our faith, [and] who for the joy that was set before Him endured the cross, despising the shame, and has sat down at the right hand of the throne of God" (Hebrews 12:2). This encapsulates the whole principle of holding onto the promise despite the difficulty of the journey. Jesus knew the reward, which was the promise of the Father. This was "the joy set before Him." He was focused on the prize so much that the circumstances never got the best of Him.

On His way to the cross, Jesus walked through betrayal, rejection, humiliation, abuse, torture, being cursed at and mocked, and being executed—some extreme circumstances indisputably. But for "the joy set before Him," for the prize, reward, and promise set before Him, Jesus endured the whole process of not just the cross, but also the journey to the cross. This included Gethsemane where He yielded His will to the Father's will, where He was also betrayed by a kiss from a friend.

The hard seasons we walk through, no matter how terrible, must be endured like Jesus did the cross, patiently waiting while the journey plays out, even if we cannot understand the whys and the hows. The key to making it through these "cross seasons" is to daily set our hearts on the promises of God, enduring the hardships and despising the shame. At times, our cross seasons are so humiliating and difficult that we can become too familiar with the smell of the shame of what's happening, allowing it to quench our zeal and fire and hope for the promise.

Be like Jesus, for He despised the shame of the cross. We see what's happening and rise above it –recognizing the reality of it, but denying the taint from entering our hearts. Remember Shadrach, Meshach, and Abednego in the time of king Nebuchadnezzar? They would not bow down to the king's golden image (see Daniel 3) and so were thrown into the fire to be burned alive. There was a fourth man who mysteriously appeared in the fire with them, having the appearance of the Son of God. They were not harmed; rather, they were brought out of the fire, and when they came out, God got the glory. Even their clothes and hair had no smell of smoke. This is what God wants to do with your story, too. He will be present in the fire, but you must walk in faith and focus on God.

There are so many more examples of this in the Bible. Joshua and Caleb were two of the twelve spies who went into Canaan to spy out the Promised Land. Of the twelve spies, only Joshua and Caleb came back believing that God would do all He said (see Numbers 14:38). The rest doubted God, holding onto their own abilities. As a result, the promise was held back from that generation and they all died in the desert, except for Caleb and Joshua. Forty years later, the Spirit of God led Joshua, who was now the leader of Israel, into and through the Promised Land, thus fulfilling His word.

Caleb made a statement that powerfully resounds with the kind of faith that inherits God's promises:

> *Now the people of Judah approached Joshua at Gilgal, and Caleb son of Jephunneh the Kenizzite said to him, "You know what the LORD said to Moses the man of God at Kadesh Barnea about you and me. I was forty years old when Moses the servant of the LORD sent me from Kadesh Barnea to explore the land. And I brought him back a report according to my convictions, but my fellow Israelites who went up with me made the hearts of the people melt in fear. I, however, followed the LORD my God wholeheartedly. So on that day Moses swore to me, 'The land on which your feet have walked will be your inheritance and that of your children forever, because you have followed the LORD my God wholeheartedly.'"*
>
> *Now then, just as the LORD promised, he has kept me alive for forty-five years since the time he said this to Moses, while Israel moved about in the wilderness. So here I am today, eighty-five years old! I am still as strong today as the day Moses sent me out; I'm just as vigorous to go out to battle now as I was then. Now give me this hill country that the LORD promised me that day. You yourself heard then that the Anakites were there and their cities were large and fortified, but, the LORD helping me, I will drive them out just as he said.*
>
> *Then Joshua blessed Caleb son of Jephunneh the Kenizzite and gave him Hebron as his inheritance. So Hebron has belonged to Caleb ever since, because he followed the LORD, the God of Israel, wholeheartedly. (Hebron used to be called*

*Kiriath Arba after Arba, who was the greatest man among
the Anakites). (Joshua 14:6–15 NIV).*

What I love about Caleb is that after forty-five years, his faith
was just as potent. He was just as determined and willing to inherit
the promise all those years later. We can see the same with Joseph
the son of Jacob, who was given dreams as a boy, but years later
through a process that included prison, came into the realization
of his destiny (see Genesis 50:20). The same with Jesus, the one
prophesied about by God the Father Himself in the Garden of Eden
(see Genesis 3:15). Jesus was the seed of the woman, the one who
would crush the serpent's head and bruise his heal, bringing about
redemption. Promises take time.

According to Habakkuk 2:2, we must write the vision down,
make it plain, and send a runner if we are going to inherit God's
promises. I personally keep all my prophecies written down or
recorded, and then I regularly reread and listen to them. This is a
powerful tool. It stirs up my faith, encourages me, and reminds me
to focus on the promises of God. We can see Paul giving Timothy,
his son in the faith, the same type of instructions, when he writes,
"This charge I commit to you, son Timothy, according to the
prophecies previously made concerning you, that by them you may
wage the good warfare" (1 Timothy 1:18).

There is a battle for your promised inheritance. Using your
prophetic promises, visions, and words from God, you must press
forward and not stop until you possess them. Recognize that a
prophetic word or promise is like a seed in the ground—it must be

nurtured so that you reap a harvest. Just like sowing and reaping regarding our giving to God, any distractions cannot be allowed into our hearts. One of the enemy's greatest goals is to wear us out to the point where we give up.

From the moment a promise is issued, the devil will begin to go to war against the expectation and faith you have in the promise. Recalling and recounting all God has told you, and declaring these things in strong faith, is the best response to the enemy's strategies. Understanding the lifeline between the promise and your faith keeps the promise alive. Let your faith arise, and you *will* possess the promise.

CHAPTER 7

UNDERSTANDING THE PROCESS OF GOD FROM HIS PERSPECTIVE

What is God's plan and heart in this whole journey of prophetic promises in each of our lives? How do we understand what He is doing or why He does what He does? To better understand the bigger picture, we need to encounter God as a master architect and creator of not just the universe, but also of our lives. He has not only created us, but He wants to progressively develop and mature us, train us, and strengthen areas of our lives to qualify us to inherit the destiny of His dreams.

God is often more focused on the outcome and inner workings of our heart than He is on the comfort of the journey. For instance, if God begins a work in a person that is intended to develop patience and perseverance, it will most likely involve waiting, which causes frustration and anxiety—the very opposite of patience. God will often use the opposite elements to forge the fruits of the Spirit within an individual.

In the same way, God will sometimes use a prophetic word to initiate the testing of our faith in order to develop the strengths and qualities the individual needs to steward the promise. Most Christians think the trail to "all the good things" He has in store for us is cotton-cushioned with no bumps or sharp edges along the way. No, this is a false belief system that has resulted in wounded, crippled Christians and people-pleasing preachers who have watered down the Word of God to draw numbers and the applause of others rather than obedience to God. Jesus said, "I have told you these things, so that in me you may have peace. In this world you will have trouble. But take heart! I have overcome the world" (John 16:33 NIV). And again:

> If you belonged to the world, it would love you as its own. As it is, you do not belong to the world, but I have chosen you out of the world. That is why the world hates you. Remember what I told you: "A servant is not greater than his master." If they persecuted me, they will persecute you also. If they obeyed my teaching, they will obey yours also. (John 15:19–20 NIV)

There are hundreds of examples throughout the Scriptures that portray the difficulties and challenges that obedient children of God go through. What benefit would athletes have if their preparation for big events was easy and without challenge? God understands that this life is a training ground for eternity, and He is actively working on the hearts of all His sons and daughters to refine us as gold in the fire. Life and the adversities on each of our pathways will be a tool in God's hands to fashion the fruits of the Spirit, maturity, endurance, and character, and most importantly, to establish faith in us all.

The journey of walking out a prophetic promise that is conceived in the spirit realm all the way until it manifests in the natural realm, is often hard. Some words will take a lifetime to come to pass, and some we may never see at all. But God is looking for faith to trust Him in the promise no matter how it looks, no matter how long it takes to come to pass.

I had the privilege of meeting Dr. Oral Roberts not long before he graduated to heaven. I listened to Dr. Roberts talk about his huge building project that he embarked on completely by faith, believing God in total obedience on a level that most of us cannot even fathom. He was building a huge multistory structure, but the project was never actually finished. In fact, he ended up selling it to a medical company for a hospital. We listened as he recounted the giant steps of faith backed with huge sums of money.

The part that impacted me so much about his story was not the fact that he embarked on the project, battled against impossible odds, and seemingly did not finish the project and had to sell the buildings. No, I was deeply impressed that he got to the end of that story and stated that He was still believing for that building because God had spoken. He was working with his son on pursuing the building as it was again on the market for sale. I was forever impacted by his story. Even over the course of time, when it looked like he had lost the property, his eyes still looked to the promise. He has been a hero to our generation in the area of faith; I see him as one of the mighty men who died in faith while still not seeing what was promised. This is scriptural and should challenge comfortable Western Christianity where everything works out perfectly in the end. It *does* work out perfectly, but in the perspective of the eternal realm where God lives, not from our shallow, short-term perspective.

Jeremiah 29:11 says that God "know[s] the thoughts I think toward you ... thoughts of peace and not of evil, to give you a future and a hope." Most Christians have been taught that this signifies that everything is going to be "peachy" in life, but this is not so. Jesus told Peter, "Very truly I tell you, when you were younger you dressed yourself and went where you wanted; but when you are old you will stretch out your hands, and someone else will dress you and lead you where you do not want to go" (John 21:18 NIV). Jesus was not speaking of a retirement home where bingo was on the schedule every Friday and Saturday. No, He was speaking of Peter's death. Jesus, the Son of God, didn't prophesy a "bless me" word over one of His closest friends. This goes against most mainstream church prophetic beliefs.

Unfortunately, I have seen many Christians, especially young ones, burn out, suffer setbacks, or even backslide because they did not understand God's ways in the working out of prophetic promises. People commonly say to me, "God told me I would be married soon, but I am still not married. That means that God either doesn't love me, has forgotten me, or I'm not good enough." This is the thinking of a person who has lost sight of God's perspective and timing. The devil has been hard at work denouncing God's love and faithfulness to that individual.

This is an ugly and powerful weapon the devil uses—rejection. It is a tool designed to wedge two people apart, creating mistrust without value or love. Satan used it in the garden with Eve eating the fruit. May I encourage you that God really isn't a man that He should lie (see Numbers 23:19)! No, He *is* the truth. If God tells you something and you know it to be true, no matter how long you may wait, keep believing Him, for He is faithful to deliver. Jesus is the author and finisher of our faith. In other words, He is the writer and the deliverer of the promises.

The Father prophetically revealed to Jesus that He was on earth for the purpose of the cross in order to redeem us all. Jesus would have not had such a clear understanding in the Garden of Gethsemane. He prayed, "Yet not my will, but yours be done" (Luke 22:42 NIV). Submission to the Father's will is crucial to obtaining the promises of God, whether it is desirable or a challenge. Trust in God, believe Him at His word, resist the devil, and allow the Spirit of God to fashion you throughout the process of waiting for the word to manifest in the natural realm.

Assumptions and expectations are dangerous when it comes to inheriting God's promises. They create an anticipated reality through the filters of our imagination, hopes, or dreams, which may not be totally clear. For instance, the day after I proposed to my wife, I took her to Disneyland. God told me that morning He was going to fast-track our marriage, and later that day we were standing in a long line behind three or four hundred people. A couple randomly walked right up to us and told us they needed to leave early and offered us their fast-track passes! We thanked them and shifted over into the fast-track lane and walked all the way to the front. I cried as I walked all the way to the front of the line because I was so touched that God was really going out of His way to confirm His word.

We moved to California from New Zealand four months after we got married to plant a church, which was quite daunting! I filtered that word through my hopes, dreams, and imaginations. I thought God was going to bless us with lots of money, success in my business, a house, nice cars, and put us in a position to be free to do what God had called us to do. This is where my filters really let me down and built an expectation quite different from what God had in mind. God wants to bless you with all kinds of good things and abundance in your life, but for us, God's version of fast-track turned out to be an intense two years after we got married. God allowed us to be under significant pressure, and thus tested us. He particularly dealt with me and gave me some good course corrections in my heart, motives, belief systems, and makeup as a whole person. My interpretation and God's intention were very different. This is exactly why we need to be soft, malleable, and open to finding out what God means and what God is doing.

Be ready to be surprised by God! The one thing I am sure of, no matter what it is that God is doing, however surprising, different or even unpleasant the process may feel, He has our long-term best interest in mind. Many times, I have turned around and looked over past seasons and thanked the Lord for correcting me, fashioning me, and even completely surprising me with the very promise I never knew I needed. The mind is such a powerful engine: if we assume that something is supposed to work out and look a certain way, and it plays out differently, we can end up rejecting the instruments God has engineered to shape, equip, and position us.

Sit back and let God be God. Play an active role, but let Him be in charge. Allow yourself the luxury of discovering all that He has planned and designed for you. This way you will arrive at destinations faster. Imagine if the children of Israel allowed God to be God and stayed in faith in the journey out of captivity. The journey from Egypt to Canaan was only supposed to take three days. Just imagine if they had avoided forty years of wandering in the wilderness. It's not our job to judge what it looks like or how long it is going to take; it's not our job to tell God how He should work in our lives. It's our job to hear His voice, to follow and obey.

Understanding God's process is directly connected to understanding God's love. God's plans and thoughts toward us are loving, nurturing, and generous. I'm loving, nurturing, and generous toward my children; because of this, I will not give them what they are not mature enough to handle. I will require that they train, study and develop to certain levels before I entrust them with certain privileges. It's not that I am not kind to them; it's that my kindness makes them wait to avoid possible damage.

God has your life perfectly planned, so listen to Him and follow His Spirit to find out His paths and His plans will unfold. It won't often make sense. That's okay, as long as we are convinced that God is good, full of grace and mercy toward us all the time. God is inviting us on a journey that He plans to use as a vehicle to grow, develop, and qualify us for the inheritance He has planned for us. God is good. In order to inherit the promises of God, we need to understand the process of God from His perspective. His ways and thoughts are much higher than ours.

CHAPTER 8

POSITIONING YOURSELF WITH A PROPHETIC WORD

When God speaks, He is inviting us to go on a journey. Most often, His words don't describe our current position or environment. Rather, He gives us a glimpse of the plans He has for us, which may seem far beyond our existing circumstances or abilities. Once God has spoken, it is difficult to know how to proceed. How do you get from where you now stand to what He has shown you? Or even worse, you assume you're ready to run before you crawl.

When God vision casts or prophesies, we get insights of where we are going, which can be inspiring and yet overwhelming. Positioning ourselves to be ready for it to come to pass is a crucial key to inheriting the vision. We must not find ourselves behind or ahead of His plan unfolding. But rather, we must go to God and seek Him until He reveals what and how we are to align ourselves toward His provision, supply, and destiny.

This is such an important aspect of the prophetic coming to pass. If God is going to open the floodgates of heaven and pour out a blessing so that we cannot contain it, then we want to be standing underneath it when it is finally poured out. This way we can catch it, possess it, and not miss what God wants to do. There is a timing, positioning, and aligning of certain things in our lives that must line up when we are walking toward a prophetic promise.

WAITING FOR GOD'S PROMISE TO COME TO PASS

when David was anointed king of Israel in 1 Samuel 16, it did not mean that he immediately became king; rather, he had a promise and needed to look for the open door toward that office. The reason he was chosen to be king is that he knew his God, and he knew that God was with him. David received the promise of being king, but he needed to wait for quite some time before it came to pass. The offer of a portion of the kingdom, a tax-free life, and the king's daughter in marriage was a step in the right direction toward the fulfillment of the promise given by a prophet years before. The promise didn't come through defeating the lion or the bear. It was offered by the king as a reward to any person who would fight and slay Goliath (see 1 Samuel 17:25). This is the reason David was so confident he was the man for the job, although he was still a boy.

Have you ever surfed or visited a surfing beach? The waves are huge pulses of water that rise out of the swell and become a wall of water moving at great speeds. Surfers sitting on their boards simply do not just "catch the wave," no, they paddle as fast as they can and need to sit in the right place on the wave to catch it and ride it. The surfer must paddle in order to increase his or her speed to match that of the wave and join the momentum; more than this, the board must be pointed in the right direction and at just the right place in the surf—not too early and not too late—in order to catch a ride. Catching a wave in surfing is quite an art, involving position, momentum, and direction. The skill that the surfer has acquired will determine how well he or she rides it.

Positioning yourself to enter a prophetic word is similar. Where you position yourself and your movements toward the promise is crucial. You need to grow into the skills that are required of you to walk into the full extent of your promise. Often we will never see the full picture of what the promise looks like until we get to the destination. This is similar to a person who knows he or she is called as a missionary to a nation where a different language is spoken. God has spoken, but the timing has not been revealed as to when it will happen. Learning the language in advance would be a wise way for that person to begin positioning him or herself to be ready when the time comes. Sitting on the sofa waiting for things to fall out of the sky, would be unwise.

BEING ALIGNED WITH GOD'S WILL

If God calls you to worship, simply showing up to your church worship practice is not enough. You will need take music lessons so that your skill and abilities are that of a level required to lead God's people into His presence. That may take years of dedication, practice, and preparation in order to enter the dream God has for you. It's not all about skill, of course; I have seen and heard some of the most talented, skilled people play and sing, but there has been no anointing on them. There needs to be personal time spent secretly with God, developing a relationship and intimacy with Him, and from there His presence and anointing can flow.

Intimacy with God is more important than the gifting or skill level of the person. Although the skill level is important, it's just dry noise that has no anointing if there is not personal intimacy with the Lord first. Many seek intimacy with God to anoint their gift or bless their endeavors, but this is a wrong motivation. We must seek God for who He is and to know Him more, and the anointing will come naturally. Then if you feel God has called you to worship, you must be prepared to commit to the time required to practice on your worship team and be submitted to the leadership in a healthy, spiritual way. Then and only then are you positioned to fully receive the prophetic word unfolded into reality.

An entirely different angle of this positioning aspect is staying where God plants you. Unfortunately, we live in a generation in which most people live their lives based on feelings and convenience. Paul said in the last days that "men would be lovers of themselves ..." (2 Timothy 3:2 NIV). Often, the Word of the Lord will cost you and be inconvenient; it's not for the faint, weak hearted, or cowardly.

For example, let's say God speaks to you and plants you in a local church under a pastor. Your obedience and faithfulness to that instruction will determine whether or not you will hear God reveal His intentions to you. Did you notice that I used the word *instruction* and not *suggestion*? Learning the fear of the Lord, which is a weighty, reverential respect of God's greatness, is a huge step of wisdom. There's no room for *creative negotiation* by removing yourself from the situation; it demands your obedience. The Scriptures instruct us in 1 Samuel 15:22 that God values obedience over sacrifice, so we should take this seriously.

If God plants you somewhere, He has put you there on purpose. He has things for you to encounter there, like healing, deliverance, teaching, encouragement, empowerment, and even enlightenment to what is unhealthy in your life. Your ability to stay faithful to those instructions will dictate your eligibility for God to use you in greater measures. This includes keeping your heart right even when leaders or members of the church hurt your feelings, speak or preach about subjects that trigger painful issues or tender places in your heart that need healing. In other situations, I've seen people who were given "exciting" opportunities elsewhere that enticed them away from God's perfect plan. They walked away to the next exciting endeavor, and I watched as they moved further and further away from their promise. Some eventually even completely drifted away from God.

This problem is the same one that Esau had in Genesis 25:29–34. Esau, in a moment of seemingly extreme hunger, traded his birthright, which was essentially his inheritance of the entire family fortune, for a mere bowl of lentil stew. I don't believe that he was *that* hungry, to the point of trading everything for one meal so easily. Esau's heart had become so familiar and flippant with the pending promise of inheritance that he ended up disdaining it. He gave it up because he had wandered in his heart from his promised position as an inheritor, instead giving it away for something that didn't last more than twenty minutes. We must always hold these prophetic promises and opportunities with a sense of awe, wonder, and anticipation. Never lose the faith and hope in what God has promised. Stay where He plants you until He clearly speaks with detailed instructions for the next steps, confirming that it's really Him and not your emotions that are speaking.

There was a season in my life that lasted more than a decade in which God had me in a harsh and even hostile environment. There were many times I didn't want to be there, but God had planted me in that community, so I was faithful. Years later God revealed His intentions and reasons, inviting me into my next season. I could have used hundreds of legitimate reasons to excuse myself from that situation, but I only had the right to obey God's instructions, not create my own path.

If we look at Malachi 3:10, which talks about giving finances to God, there is something we can learn here about staying faithful to God's vision and where He planted us:

> *"Bring all the tithes into the storehouse,*
>
> *That there may be food in My house,*
>
> *And try Me now in this,"*

Says the LORD of hosts,

"If I will not open for you the windows of heaven

And pour out for you such blessing

That there will not be room enough to receive it."

What are these windows of heaven? If a window of heaven was to open for us, we would want to be close by. In the same way, if a relief plane was dropping several crates of supplies by parachute into a war-struck or famine-plagued territory, the people it was intended for would want to be at the drop zone to receive it. We must view God's promises in a similar way. When God speaks, it's our job to move toward the positions that will set us in a place to receive. In each situation, however, we must be led by the Spirit of God and not be hasty or presumptuous.

Always remember the story of Jonah, the prophet, whom God instructed to go and prophesy against the wicked city of Nineveh. Jonah, instead of obeying and positioning himself with the instructions of God, ran in the opposite direction, hitching a ride on a sailing ship. God caused a great storm to beat on the ship to the point that everyone thought they were going to die. Jonah came to his senses and claimed responsibility; he had the crew throw him into the water where a great fish swallowed him, and in its belly he remained for three days and three nights. Eventually, after what must have felt like an eternity in hell, he was spat out on the beach near Nineveh and made his way toward the place God had instructed him. Now positioned correctly, he was able to fulfill

God's will. Always remember that God's plan and instructions may not always be convenient or even remotely in your comfort zone.

God's dream and blueprint requires cooperation and involvement. If you are confused as to what you should do and how you should position yourself with something God has said, begin to ask God to show you how you should move toward His dream. Keep asking until He reveals the path. If God has called you to be a minister, you may start serving in the church in an area that may seem insignificant. My story has years of this type of thing, serving by cleaning up, maintenance, weekly setup of the sanctuary, parking cars, and security duties. Some would think, "Oh, you're called for more; your gift is above these tasks." But all the while, I could feel God's pleasure and preparation as I positioned myself toward what He had shown me. Years later I began to walk in the promises, only to receive more promises that would cause a new set of positioning required. This life of following God's promises is an exciting journey, and God is inviting us to position ourselves to receive a prophetic word.

CHAPTER 9

BIRTHING PROPHETIC PROMISES

Birthing a promise that God has given is much like birthing a baby. There is a moment of conception, which is the moment the word of the Lord is planted like a seed into the soil of your heart. Then there is a gestation period, or a pregnancy season, which is like a seed of promise growing and housed inside of your heart and mind, hidden from the world but alive to you. And then there is the time where you give birth and see the promise of God in the natural realm.

When my wife was pregnant, there were times when the babies in her belly were sleeping and she just had a bump on her stomach, but then there were other times when the babies were awake and moving and kicking, so much so that we could see their little hands and feet pushing out against her stomach. There are times when promises seem dormant, when nothing has seemed to happen in a while and God seemingly has not spoken, But all the same, we recognize the pregnancy of the promise within us.

When John the Baptist was still in Elizabeth's womb, Elizabeth met with Mary who was pregnant at that time with Jesus. The Scriptures tell us that John leaped inside the womb in the presence of the yet unborn Savior (see Luke 1:41). Although there can be seasons of quietness, there can also be events and seasons in which the pregnant promises within us begin to leap as God stirs them up. Even though they're not yet birthed and manifested to the outside world, they are nevertheless real—it's just a matter of time until they are birthed.

Then comes the day that every mother both awaits in anticipation for and fears to some extent. Birthing is no casual experience. It is the transition of what started as a seed, grew into a form, and became so big it could no longer be contained inside of the mother. The child must be birthed and enter the outside world.

The birthing process is a laboring process that I am not even going to attempt to claim I understand. Women are simply amazing and are crafted by God to be conduits of this life-giving, birthing process. When I was in the delivery room with my wife expecting our firstborn, we went from just two people—Rebekah and myself, to suddenly, in a moment, becoming three as our son joined us.

Birthing prophetic promises is much the same. The promise is in you, you have believed, it has grown, you have positioned yourself and waited for God's timing, and then suddenly, in one moment, it manifests. Sometimes you see it coming, while at other times it will catch you by surprise. Either way, the second it arrives, everything is forever changed.

FAITH AND WORKS

Faith and works, or faith backed with actions, are two equally essential ingredients to see the promises translate from the spirit realm into the natural realm. Many Christians believe that it is simply enough to believe and declare that something will come to pass and it will. For instance, I've known several different people who declared for years that they would be millionaires because God had spoken to them and through others prophetically. Yet they lived in poverty for years, mainly due to a lack of wisdom and lack of hard work. There is more involved in inheriting promises than faith and hope. James 2:18 reminds us, "But someone will say, 'you have faith, and I have works.' Show me your faith without your works, and I will show you my faith by my works." People who commit their hearts to faith without works are missing the whole point.

If we are going to believe God at His word and hope with all sincerity for His promises, then we must back up our faith with works that are in agreement to that faith and hope. In essence, we need to step out of the boat and move toward the promise in the natural as best as we can, not just in the spirit. People who only have faith and do not couple their belief with works are lazy and live in fear. A lifestyle that waits but does not work is a type of spiritual welfare, an entitlement mentality. The Bible says that if we don't work, we won't eat (see 2 Thessalonians 3:10)! This is not to suggest that we depend on our works; but works are necessary as an outworking of our faith.

If a farmer wants a glass of fresh milk and looks out his kitchen window at his dairy cow grazing in the paddock with udders bulging, says to himself, "I'm believing for that glass of milk; I know it's mine. I own that cow. I can't physically see the milk yet but I know it's mine. I hope I get a glass of that milk today." Faith without works will never drink that milk, because it's purely a belief with no action. Faith *with* works will go outside, set up a stool and bucket, and begin to milk the cow. This action is works!

Do everything in your ability to stand strong, committed to the promise for which you're believing. Faith without works is only spiritual laziness, going through the motions without walking the walk. It's all good and well to have high hopes and dreams, but God is looking for us to put our money where our mouth is so He can bless us. After all, it's the Father's good pleasure to give us the kingdom!

PRAYING A PROMISE THROUGH

There are varying forms of prayer, each with a particular application. For instance, there are heartfelt intimate prayers where we share the deep places of our hearts with God. Then there are prayers of intercession, where we pray on behalf of people and circumstances. At other times there is a great burden and we come before the throne of God to plead our case. What I want to focus on here is prayer that prays through from the conception of a prophetic promise to the moment of its realization. Prayer is not a strange chore reserved for the intercessors in a church. If someone believes this, then he or she needs to be saved. God is a God of relationship and conversation. Prayer is essentially conversation with God.

Effective prayer begins when the individual is absolutely convinced that what he or she believes is a promise from God. From that place, we need to pray without ceasing while being led by the Holy Spirit. This type of prayer is tenacious and determined; it contends with heaven to deliver the promise and confronts hell to get out of the way and to bow to the will of Father God.

At times, prayer can be like the laboring and travailing of a birthing process. We must build a lifestyle that intentionally prays daily to lay hold of what God has promised and that does not quit until the promised word of the Lord is inherited. Once we are certain of what God has promised, we have an obligation to pray it through until it comes about, no matter the time frame.

There's a fine line between waiting and positioning yourself for a prophetic promise, and striving in your own abilities to obtain that promise. When patience gives way to unwillingness to wait on God's perfect timing, you may be tempted to think that God needs your help. This is not healthy or helpful. So you begin to force yourself into environments, situations, and even relationships in the attempt to hurry the process along. The problem in doing this is that the strength of your own ability does not please or impress God. In fact, it pollutes His plans , causing detours, extensions, and even disqualifications.

God won't share His glory with any person; it belongs exclusively to Him. When we assume to foolishly assist God with our childish, forceful, and ambitious strength, trusting in our own abilities, we are operating in pride. This blocks God's channel of provision and delivery, because we are too afraid to genuinely rest and abide in God's ability, trusting His heart for us.

Strength in our own abilities, also referred to as strength in our flesh, is a rebellious dismissal of God's greatness. Instead, we are trying to imitate God and are deluded into thinking we are our own provider. Whatever you push your way into will drain you of your energy to maintain. Rest in God and trust His process, for no one truly wants to pay the huge cost of maintaining something in his or her own abilities. Allow God to promote you and bring His promises to pass in His timing. Proverbs tells us, "The blessing of the LORD makes one rich, and He adds no sorrow with it" (Proverbs 10:22). Striving always produces sorrow.

The question must be asked, "How do I birth my own prophetic promises in God's way?" This is the right question to ask. It is essential to understand that both of us (God and us) have roles to play in these processes. Knowing what our job is and what God's job is, causes us to have understanding and an intense focus.

We can rest secure when we allow Him to work out the delivery and timing of the promise. When we surrender to this fact, a great peace that surpasses our understanding becomes available. In turn, when we know what our role is, we can then focus on it and become highly diligent and faithful until the promise is delivered.

ASSISTING THE BIRTHING OF YOUR PROMISES

Don't allow yourself to cross the line by pushing your own idea of what God has said or you will sabotage it every single time. Let's briefly look at a few important points that will assist you in the birthing of your promises and destiny.

WAGE WAR WITH THE PROPHECIES GIVEN TO YOU

To assist in birthing the promises God has given, you need to learn to wage war with the prophecies given to you (see 1 Timothy 1:18; 4:14–15). When God speaks, expect a battle. The enemy hears God's words and often will attack our environment to cause us to back up, lose faith, or be intimidated. Our response must be in the language of faith and agreement with God's word. There may be a battle; you may even feel as though all hell has declared war against you, but you must calm your mind and emotions, and trust God. His words always come to pass and deliver the promise if you simply and stubbornly hold on and believe Him.

RESTING AND WAITING ON GOD'S TIMING

Rest and wait on God's timing by being content with where you are, while at the same time exercising faith for where you are going. While you wait, don't become discouraged when it doesn't happen in the timing you expected. Surrender your need to be in control.

Have you ever seen one of those scenes in a film where the man is sinking in quicksand? Quicksand is a wet sand that can swallow you up. The interesting thing about quicksand is that when you are stuck in it, the more you struggle to get out, the deeper you sink. The same is true while waiting on God—the more you struggle and strive and stress (in your own strength), the deeper you sink into frustration and turmoil. There is so much peace in trusting God's perfect timing. Find that place in your waiting seasons.

PRAYING IN THE PROMISE

Declare the promise repeatedly, recite it to God, remind Him that you believe Him, and know that He will be faithful. The value of consistent prayer must be a daily practice in your life. Before Jesus stepped into the most crucial season of His earthly life, He was in the Garden of Gethsemane lifting up deep, powerful, and even vehement prayers to the Father. He prayed the will of the Father and submitted His own will in order to save us all on Calvary. We must learn to pray the various types of prayers: prayers of submission, prayers of repentance, prayers of inquiring about God's will, and prayers of calling heaven to come into our environment. For prayer is what will help us obtain the promises of God.

EQUIPPING AND PREPARING YOURSELF

Equip and prepare yourself for what you believe God has told you to do so you can be ready for the promise. For instance, in the previous chapter, I mentioned the importance of learning a language or skill set in advance so you are equipped for the season ahead, whatever that may be. If you were to compete in a sport, you would not watch movies and eat junk food every day; you would learn the sport, all the rules and parameters, and you would train and discipline your body and mind so that you became an expert. You would do this to such an extent that when you had the opportunity to step into the competitive level, you would be prepared. We must also approach God's destiny for our lives in much the same way.

There are probably practical areas for which you can prepare yourself. If God has told you that He is going to give you wealth, then simply dreaming about the promise and hoping it comes together is a fantasy. It takes a diligent and consistent work ethic, as well as a savings plan, and much wisdom for you to be prepared for the promise of wealth. God is such a wise "investor" of promises. He is not going to put money in pockets that have holes in them. Sew up the holes in the pockets of your life so that you will be a wise investment.

WORSHIP

Worship is one of the great ways to rest in the grace and peace of God while we wait for His promises to come about. Get lost in the romance and majesty of God's goodness. We must always remember that the prophetic promise is not our god, our source of provision, or even our identity. God alone fulfills these. Worshiping Him keeps everything in perspective while we wait on His goodness to be fulfilled in our lives.

STAY FRUITFUL

Stay fruitful in your current situation while you wait on the next season. Bloom where you are planted. My wife and I have seen so many people shut down whole aspects of their lives, putting all kinds of things on hold while they wait for God to bring about what is next. I've had people tell me, "I'm not going to be involved in any serving around my church or even sharing the gospel and saving souls, because I just want to focus on this one promise that God made, and I don't feel like I should do anything else until it happens." The word *feel* is a dangerous one. It's an expression of people's emotions, not a representation of the word of the Lord. This "put everything on hold" belief system is not from God.

If you look at Adam in the garden, the Bible records that "the LORD God took the man and put him in the Garden of Eden to work it and take care of it" (Genesis 2:15). Adam was obedient to God, caring and tending the garden, faithful in the sphere of responsibility God had given him, serving with excellence. Genesis 2:18 states that "the LORD God said, 'It is not good for the man to be alone. I will make a helper suitable for him.'" In that moment,

God brought Adam into his next season by putting him to sleep and taking one of his ribs to create Eve, his wife. While we wait on the promises God has given, we must not become distracted and discontent, or even offended. Be found faithful in your area of serving or responsibility; let your life speak of faithfulness and fruitfulness to God; win souls, heal the sick, disciple people in the measure you are qualified to; and do all of these as an act of love to God. You will get His attention and He will step in at the appointed time, like He did for Adam, and your season will change.

STAY HUMBLE

At times, certain prophetic words are so grand and great that they can appeal to our pride and ego. Never allow those moments to enter your heart. Stay humble. James reminds us, "Humble yourself before the Lord, and He will lift you up" (James 4:10 NIV). Humility is a fragrance that attracts the attention and presence of God. It will also safeguard you from sabotaging your own journey with pride.

Repeatedly approach God and ask Him for strategies on how you should wait, proceed, behave, speak, and navigate while walking toward His perfect will. Never just hear God once on these strategies and trust that everything will work out. Have you ever driven with a GPS? As you progress through your journey and approach your destination, the GPS will give you updated and more specific instructions to ensure you arrive at your destination on time. The same is true with God. There is a constant updating and advising as you approach your prophetic fulfillment. Continually inquire of God, even if it seems monotonous. A single strategic piece of advice will change everything!

CHAPTER 10

INQUIRING OF THE LORD

Inquiring of the Lord is something we must do as a result of realizing our absolute need of His assistance and direction for our lives. Here is a portion of Scripture that has meant a great deal to me on this subject:

> Then I [Ezra] proclaimed a fast there at the river of Ahava, that we might humble ourselves before our God, to seek from Him the right way for us and our little ones and all our possessions. For I was ashamed to request of the king an escort of soldiers and horsemen to help us against the enemy on the road, because we had spoken to the king, saying, 'The hand of our God is upon all those for good who seek Him, but His power and His wrath are against all those who forsake Him.' So we fasted and entreated our God for this, and He answered our prayer. (Ezra 8:21–23)

Inquiring of the Lord is an essential part of any child of God's life. It demands humility of the great and small, the beginner and the experienced, because to find out the Master's plan, one must recognize his or her need, and place a high value on God's direction regardless of expectations or preferences. The Bible tells us, "Surely He scorns the scornful, but gives grace to the humble" (Proverbs 3:34). Grace, the potent empowering gift from God that causes us to function in whatever facet He has called us to function, comes only to the humble. And we need to remember that humility is pleasing to God; He draws near when we position our hearts and minds in this way.

Inquiring of God means that we seek out His counsel, heart, plan, and strategies for our lives and communities. Proverbs 25:2 says, "It is the glory of God to conceal a matter; to search out a matter is the glory of kings" (NIV). God does not always lay out in plain sight every secret and the right path we are to take. Many times, we find ourselves facing a crossroads, a decision, or challenge in which the best strategy is not easily apparent. And just making an educated guess based on experience is often foolishness.

Always remember that we have an enemy, the devil, who desires to disqualify, steal, and sabotage our journeys away from God's best for us. Proverbs again reminds us, "There is a way that seems right to a man, but its end is the way of death" (Proverbs 14:12). It's easy to take control of our destiny and decisions, assuming we know how to steer our own ship. How many times were we so convinced that we knew the right decision to make in a situation? We were so sure that our insight, experience, and wisdom were sufficient to make the right decision. But just when we had made our decision, a terrible curve ball came out of nowhere and shocked us as it sabotaged our plans, and we were left devastated.

We all have had these moments when we've been outsmarted and put in a weaker position because we didn't have the foresight to see into the future. This is exactly why we need to humble ourselves and pursue the whole counsel of God. God sees the end of a time line before the beginning; He is so amazing that He can view every moment in time at the same instant. He is the best counselor, advisor, and coach we could ever imagine. We must put a value on His wisdom, insight, and foresight and seek it out.

Proverbs gives us wisdom that should be applied to our lives:

Trust in the LORD with all your heart,

And lean not on your own understanding;

In all your ways acknowledge Him,

And He shall direct your paths.

Do not be wise in your own eyes;

Fear the LORD and depart from evil. (Proverbs 3:5–7)

Humility and dependency are attractive to God. The Scriptures tell us, "But without faith it is impossible to please Him, for he who comes to God must believe that He is, and that He is a rewarder of those who diligently seek Him" (Hebrews 11:6). Walking in genuine faith requires both humility and dependency. It's a conscious realization of our total need of God's greatness and goodness, His wisdom and leading. David inquired of the Lord regularly throughout his lifetime; there were times when God would tell him to wait, times when God would tell him to move, times when God would say no, and times when God would say yes.

In modern periods, military troops on the ground in combat have a tactical person using real-time satellite imaging to give instructions, intel, and strategies to the special forces persons through an in-ear communication system. The Intel person can see the whole picture from above, while an individual soldier on the ground can only see his immediate surroundings. The intelligence person can see behind walls and even what is coming down the road from a distance. The ground soldier must rely 100 percent on the instructions and the advice of the Intel.

So it is with God. He sees everything with a perspective unlimited by time; He sees everything from start to finish in the same moment, while we can only see our immediate surroundings at any given moment. Making decisions on immediate surroundings can be a gamble at best, and so many times our decisions are mere guesswork. Wouldn't it be wiser to pray and ask God for wisdom first and avoid needing a way of escape from a bad situation later?

Let's closely study one instance (of so many) in David's life, just after Saul had died and David was king over Israel. Read closely and consider these weighty events, the pending threat, and the details of what David did.

> Now when the Philistines heard that they had anointed David king over Israel, all the Philistines went up to search for David. And David heard of it and went down to the stronghold. The Philistines also went and deployed themselves in the Valley of Rephaim. So David inquired of

*the LORD, saying, "Shall I go up against the Philistines? Will
You deliver them into my hand?"*

*And the LORD said to David, "Go up, for I will doubtless
deliver the Philistines into your hand."*

*So David went to Baal Perazim, and David defeated them
there; and he said, "The LORD has broken through my enemies
before me, like a breakthrough of water." Therefore he called
the name of that place Baal Perazim. And they left their
images there, and David and his men carried them away.*

*Then the Philistines went up once again and deployed
themselves in the Valley of Rephaim. Therefore David
inquired of the LORD, and He said, "You shall not go up;
circle around behind them, and come upon them in front of
the mulberry trees. And it shall be, when you hear the sound
of marching in the tops of the mulberry trees, then you shall
advance quickly. For then the LORD will go out before you
to strike the camp of the Philistines." And David did so, as
the LORD commanded him; and he drove back the Philistines
from Geba as far as Gezer. (2 Samuel 5:17–25)*

Now when the Philistines heard that they had anointed David
king over Israel, all the Philistines went up to search for David. And
David heard of it and went down to the stronghold. (2 Samuel 5:17)

David was threatened by the enemy gathering to come up against
him. His first response once he heard about it was to go down to the
stronghold. He went to a fortress where he would be safe. This has
prophetic significance. Do you remember the scripture, "The name of
the LORD is a strong tower, the righteous run into it and they are safe?"
(Proverbs 18:10). This act of running into the stronghold is exactly

what we should do when presented with a threat from the enemy. We run into the presence of God, because that is where we are the safest.

We see immediately by reading further in the passage that "the Philistines also went and deployed themselves in the Valley of Rephaim" (2 Samuel 5:18). Isn't it amazing that even when we run to God as our refuge, it appears that the enemy will still set up in battle array and deploy his forces against us? It is in these moments that we must calmly and patiently wait in the presence of God, not doing anything rashly or in a haste, because the enemy will always take advantage of us if we do.

Then we see one of the reasons why David was the greatest king whom God referred to as a man after His own heart: "So David inquired of the LORD, saying, 'shall I go up against the Philistines? Will You deliver them into my hand?'" (2 Samuel 5:19). I find this so beautiful. David was a feared, seasoned warrior, trained in military tactics and strategies. His renown exceeded Sauls as the people chanted in earlier years, "Saul has slain his thousands, and David his tens of thousands" (1 Samuel 18:7). We do not see a coward running to hide in a tower and then begging God to save him; rather, we see a man who had a military plan already forming. He asked God if He could go up against the enemy, and if God would deliver the enemy into his hands.

God responded to the inquiry with wisdom and insight: The Lord said to David, "Go up, for I will doubtless deliver the Philistines into your hand" (2 Samuel 5:18). David, with the full confidence that God had already told him the outcome, went out to meet his adversary:

"So David went to Baal Perazim, and David defeated them there; and he said, 'The LORD has broken through my enemies before me, like a breakthrough of water.' Therefore he called the name of that place Baal Perazim. And they left their images there, and David and his men carried them away" (2 Samuel 5:20–21).

After that victory, the enemy made yet another attempt to attack David: "Then the Philistines went up once again and deployed themselves in the Valley of Rephaim. Therefore David inquired of the LORD" (2 Samuel 5:22–23). I love that David immediately went back to God. He didn't just rely on the previous word that God said, but he came back for fresh instructions. This is wisdom that we all should heed.

Now we see a completely different answer from God: "And He said, 'You shall not go up; circle around behind them, and come upon them in front of the mulberry trees. And it shall be, when you hear the sound of marching in the tops of the mulberry trees, then you shall advance quickly. For then the LORD will go out before you to strike the camp of the Philistines" (2 Samuel 5:23–24).

It is good caution not to assume that what God said previously will be the same now. Haste is one of the greatest destiny robbers. Religion tends to predict God's advice based on past experiences and encounters. God is the God of relationship. We need to come to Him daily for leading and instruction, leaning not on our own understanding. God's instructions revealed positioning in the mulberry trees, timing when he heard marching in the tops of the trees, instruction to advance quickly against his enemy, and finally that God would go out in front of them and strike the enemy's camp. Inquiring of the Lord is very crucial. We have an invitation to ask the architect of the universe for advice and instructions.

"And David did so, as the LORD commanded him; and he drove back the Philistines from Geba as far as Gezer" (2 Samuel 5:25). David obeyed the Lord's instructions and had an overwhelming victory, breaking the enemy's back. David inquired of the Lord and then obeyed. Even though David had natural abilities and strengths, his trust, dependency, and reliance was completely on God's leading. I encourage you to use David as a model for your life. There's never anything that we cannot ask God about, whether it be a huge, weighty decision or something that seems insignificant. God wants to be involved in every part of our lives. He is not just a planner of all the big details, but His plans and dreams go down to the most microscopic detail. Of course, we have a free will, but God wants us to freely give Him the lordship of every area of our lives, choices, and journeys.

Find out from God who you are and what He has planned for your life. Become confident in who you are and what God is showing you: "So then faith comes by hearing, and hearing by the word of God" (Romans 10:17). As you understand who you are in God, confidence will come and as your confidence increases, you will bear more fruit. Inquiring of the Lord is a crucial part of our journey moving forward, to living out the destiny for which God created you.

CHAPTER 11

LIVING IN AGREEMENT WITH GOD

God's promises are God's plans, which means He oversees the whole of our lives. It's the greater person inviting the lesser person into the greater person's dream and vision. For us to see His blueprint unfold, we must partner with Him. We take ownership when we agree completely with God's vision. It becomes our vision. Two people working together require agreement in words, heart motives, plans, and actions. This is why Amos asks, "Can two walk together, unless they are agreed?" (Amos 3:3). Hearing and understanding the spirit of prophecy is really the voiced heart of God. By nature, God will invite us to live in agreement with Him.

The Word of God tells us plainly in Proverbs 29:18, "Where there is no vision, the people perish: but he that keepeth the law, happy is he" (KJV). The Bible also explains, "My people are destroyed for lack of knowledge..." (Hosea 4:6 KJV). These are two statements that describe the state of a person's life, path, purpose, and direction, a person who does not listen to God's voice. Without the input of God's voice, people revert to their own idea of wisdom, or, just as bad, they take gambles and wild guesses in their decision-making. I liken this mind-set to Russian roulette, which is a reckless mentality.

Russian roulette is a deranged "game" in which people take a single bullet, load it into a revolver, spin the chamber, point the gun at their own head, and pull the trigger. It was taking a lethal risk—a gamble with the participant's own life. When people take their destiny into their own hands by guessing at decisions or being led by emotions or desires, they are taking their own life in their hands with the same lunacy as someone who plays Russian roulette. This causes them to miss God's best. We want to be a people who see, hear, and follow God's plan, which clearly sets out a map for us to follow.

Once we hear His voice, God may speak a promise, commandment, or a vision over an aspect of our life, or even something that we may not want to do. We need to be like Jesus in the Garden of Gethsemane, when He conversed with the Father about His destiny at Calvary. Whatever God reveals to us, we then have a choice to make, to either live in agreement or in disagreement with God's word or plan.

When it comes to group or personal promises and prophetic revelations, God's specific prophetic word or promises can only come to pass if we agree with Him and move forward with the eyes of faith toward the promise. The kingdom of heaven is based and built upon *unity* and agreement. To explain it more simply, the Father, Son, and Spirit are *one,* which means they always agree and work together. In Acts 2, all the disciples were all in one accord (or unity) in the upper room while praying, waiting for the promise of God's Spirit to come and empower them.

To see the manifestation of the will, plans, and purposes of God, we must see through the eyes of faith to obtain God's heart on a matter, *then* adjust our hearts if necessary to believe and agree with God's ultimate plan. When these are in place, then God can deliver the promise, even if it takes time. Find out God's will for you, whether it's a big or small decision or dream, and agree with His heart! After we hear God's voice or He has revealed His will to us, we should double check and verify that what we heard is undoubtedly from God. God requires our agreement in order for His plan to unfold; He is looking for people who will become partners with Him.

When God reveals His will over my life, it's initially news to me and it will sometimes even be unexpected or shocking. I would never imagine that these were a part of my destiny, but God thought otherwise. There are other times when God has revealed something to me that I didn't want to hear. The truth is that we live in a generation that only seems to want to hear desirable or exciting prophetic words and promises.

Paul warned Timothy about this: "For the time will come when people will not put up with sound doctrine. Instead, to suit their own desires, they will gather around them a great number of teachers to say what their itching ears want to hear" (2 Timothy 4:3 NIV). Paul warned us about this generation's flaws. We must be aware of these and adopt kingdom values, not generational cultural trends. This is especially true as the world hurtles toward an ever-increasingly rebellious culture, opposing God. Unfortunately this culture is seeping into corners of the church, watering down the potency of God's intended design for His sons and daughters.

In my relationship with my wife, I do not want her to say only pleasant things to me and keep the bad things to herself. My wife is the sweetest person I know, but at times she needs to share her heart with me about practical things that are bothering her, or bad news she received or views she has, which may shed light on problems that we both need to be aware of. I am a richer man because she freely shares her heart with me—both exciting things and challenging things.

The same must be true in our relationship with God. If our idea of the prophetic is only about exciting plans of how great we will be and how amazing we are, then we have much learning to do. If we try to limit God with those ideas, then we are assuming to control the God of the universe. Let's look at two examples from the Scriptures to establish a right belief system in this area.

In the book of Genesis, God looked on the earth and was displeased with humanity's state, to the point of wanting to destroy everyone, except Noah and his family. Genesis records:

> The earth also was corrupt before God, and the earth was filled with violence. So God looked upon the earth, and indeed it was corrupt; for all flesh had corrupted their way on the earth.

> And God said to Noah, "The end of all flesh has come before Me, for the earth is filled with violence through them; and behold, I will destroy them with the earth. Make yourself

an ark of gopher wood; make rooms in the ark, and cover it
inside and outside with pitch" (Genesis 6:11–14).

God visited Noah and told him that He was preparing to destroy the population of the world. The destruction of his community was not exactly exciting news. But God asked Noah to build a ship to save the animals and his family. It's a good thing Noah agreed with God and obeyed—doing exactly what God asked him to do.

We know that Jesus is the ultimate and perfect example of living in agreement with the Father. We read in John's gospel about how Jesus agreed with the Father while He lived out His life on the earth:

Then Jesus answered and said to them, "Most assuredly, I
say to you, the Son can do nothing of Himself, but what He
sees the Father do; for whatever He does, the Son also does in
like manner. For the Father loves the Son, and shows Him all
things that He Himself does; and He will show Him greater
works than these, that you may marvel" (John 5:19–20).

Jesus lived in perfect agreement and harmony with the Father, which was why He demonstrated the kingdom. Although Jesus was aware of His appointment to be the sacrifice for humankind at Calvary prior to His time praying in the Garden of Gethsemane, it was as if the Father revealed to a greater extent what was to unfold. Jesus, although He was the Son of God, still had His own will. There was a struggle in the garden that night—Jesus desired another way. He prayed, "Father, if you are willing, take this cup from me; yet not my will, but yours be done" (Luke 22:42 NIV). At that moment, Jesus came into agreement and aligned himself with the Father and the plan began to unfold.

Living in agreement with God's vision and dream means two things. First, it is agreeing with the prophetic vision or promise so much that I begin to adopt it. Although it will always be God's plan and dream first, I take so much ownership of it that it becomes my own too, and I begin to push toward it so that I may inherit it.

Second, while walking toward the promise, we must always remember that every other area and part of our lives must line up with God's word and ways as well. Walking in willful sin and rebellion can cause blockages. In order to inherit God's promises, we must walk worthy of our high calling and honor God's requirements.

This grand process that God has us all walking out can seem long and difficult at times even to the point of being disheartened. But it's not what it appears. Even when the process hurts or is delayed longer than we hope, when it costs us more than we could ever imagine, He will not fail us. Stay the course and hold fast to the promises of God, for the success of our process requires our unwavering agreement with God's plan, even when we don't understand His reasoning or logic. Only believe and you will see God's goodness in your life.

CHAPTER 12

FAITH AND OBEDIENCE TO INHERIT THE PROMISES

The writer of Hebrews reminds us, "Now faith is the substance of things hoped for, the evidence of things not seen" (Hebrews 11:1). This well-known verse describes faith as seeing what has not yet materialized in our reality with so much conviction that it is as if it already existed. Faith is the vehicle by which God transports every good blessing, resource, or breakthrough that we will ever require from His abundant supplies, from heaven into our natural world.

The eyes of faith see what has been promised by God, and the prophetic assists with this. Seeing into the reality of God's promises helps strengthen our faith, because in seeing a glimpse into God's promises, we are able to anchor our hope and engage our faith, pulling the manifestation of the promise toward us. What God speaks to us may seem impossible. We imagine the reality through the eyes of faith. God is in the habit of making, creating, and providing from nothing: "By faith we understand that the worlds were framed by the word of God, so that the things which are seen were not made of things which are visible" (Hebrew 11:3).

It's not that we always see visions of the future, but rather that when God speaks destiny and promise to us, we become so focused on the destination that we can almost touch and taste it. This will cause us to grasp a picture in our hearts and minds of all God is offering. We become so captured by what we see in faith, we will do all that we must to see the vision fulfilled. In order to see into the spirit realm, and understand God's voice, we must see only through the eyes of faith. The eyes of faith are really the key to the door into the room where we can hear and interact with God's voice. We can only see the vision of God if we are in faith!

Imagine how differently the Bible would read if the twelve spies Israel sent into Canaan had seen through the eyes of faith! Now imagine if you had been 100 percent in faith for the last season of your life—there would be a different outcome because only more of God's plans would have come to pass, because *only* faith obtains the blessing.

The opposite of the eyes of faith is seeing with the eyes of fear, doubt, and unbelief. The moment fear is present, even in seed form, we cannot see through the eyes of faith any longer. Fear dims the eyes and causes the "lawyer" of doubt and unbelief to plead a convincing case against God's plans in the courtroom of our minds. The flesh wars against the Spirit, which is why in the pursuit of

God's best for us, we *must* take captive every thought that tries to float through our minds. Guard your eye gate to prevent fear from entering or things contrary to God's will established in your mind. War for victory over the threat of the spirit of fear. Live in faith, see in faith, and walk in faith!

God has conditions to His promises. The promises contained in the Bible were dependent on the people's response of obedience in order for them to inherit what was offered. What God is asking of us is our obedience. Obedience is not a statement but a response directly related to our submission to His lordship over our lives. Obedience coupled with faith is the equation that inherits the promises of God.

Every promise or prophetic word has an action or practical response requirement attached to it, much like a conditional contract. This is faith and works operating together, much like James teaches in his writings, that "faith without works is dead" (James 2:18), or believing in something but doing nothing about it is void and empty. He goes on to write, "I will show you my faith by my works" (James 2:26). Many believe that once they receive a word, vision, dream, or promise from God, they can take their place sitting on their sofa and simply waiting for the promise to be fulfilled. This is not so.

God made a promise to the children of Israel while they stood on the banks of the Jordan. Believing the promise was simply not enough to possess Canaan. No, they needed to put their faith and works together. They did not get these aligned together when they first left the bondage of Egypt, but forty years later they did. They both trusted in God and took the actions in faith—they had to battle to claim the promise of the territories God had promised.

Simply walking in the right direction is the beginning of your expression of obedience. No, you will have to fight; you will have to battle. You will not fight flesh and blood, but you will fight against forces of darkness and principalities that war against the will of God coming to pass in your life. Satan and his demons seek to rob, kill, and destroy you. And sometimes the devil places a greater value on the promises of God than we do. If you are *really* going to walk into your Promised Land, especially if it is going to be a threat to Satan's kingdom, you will have a fight ahead. But rest assured because God is with you!

In Canaan, there were walled and fortified cities, armies, and giants. It is easy to be overwhelmed when facing new adversaries. However when we face these giants, however, we must always remember that although unseen, God is standing right at our side with all His power, love, and comfort, pointing the way and encouraging us along. Our job is to look Jesus in the eyes, like Peter on the water, not at the waves. When we feel all hell coming against us, we only need to stay calm and stand firm; it's easy to let fear get the better of us, but it's all a smokescreen. Satan is terrified that we are walking into the blessing of God's inheritance for our lives, and in doing so, gaining greater faith, stripping his kingdom, and plundering hell.

Every time God blesses you and you walk into it, you take up a stronger strategic position for extending our Father's kingdom, which ultimately is about souls being saved. Hold fast, the attack you feel as you stand in faith moving toward your promise is Satan's best attempt to rob you of God's blessing and inheritance which is yours by birthright. If you notice that when Jericho's city walls fell, or when Goliath was killed, plunder, land, and treasure always followed—not to mention breakthrough, freedom, and elimination of the enemy's threats.

A promise from God is an invitation to walk through the process until breakthrough comes. It is not always an easy fight, but concerning weighty things that affect the kingdom, it usually is a battle. In these situations, humble yourself before the Lord, believe Him at His word, no matter what false reality or facade the devil uses to derail you. Stand firm and you will inherit! Always remember that one person and God is the majority, no matter what the circumstances look like.

Every time God invites you into prophetic promise and destiny, He is also looking to reap growth and development in you. He is such an avid investor into our lives; He is looking to transform us. People have an entitlement mentality in our culture and we often struggle to come out from under it, but come out we must.

One passage that really stands out to me in this area is Deuteronomy 28. This entire chapter demonstrates God's requirements as participants in His promises. This is what God spoke to Moses regarding all those who were about to enter the Promised Land of Canaan. Joshua, the successor of Moses, would lead the people of Israel into the Promised Land; I'm sure the words Moses relayed from God would have resonated in Joshua's spirit.

The core of this prophetic message was, "If you obey all I have instructed you, then these blessings will come upon you. But if you disobey, then you will live under curses." God wasn't only talking about the blessing of inheriting the Promised Land; He was instructing them on how to behave when they got there.

Many of us tend to have a mentality of a kid waiting for a reward from his parents. We are on our best behavior right up to the point of receiving the gift, and then all our efforts go out the window and we are consumed with the gift. We must never let all our effort and discipline go when we inherit the promise. The way we walk after we inherit the promise will be observed even more closely once we have the promise. Always remember, "For everyone to whom much is given, from him much will be required" (Luke 12:48).

God is concerned with every detail of our lives He is looking at the condition of our hearts as well as our motivations. It is through faith and obedience that we inherit the promises of God.

CHAPTER 13

GOD HAS THE RIGHT TO CHANGE WHAT WE THINK IS THE PLAN

As human beings, we can become entitled and strong willed when we think we know what God has said to us. This strong will can be a powerful asset, but it can also work against us at times. It is really the perfect description of faith in action. Faith claims something as your own and becomes stubbornly determined that this is the case. However, if one small detail is out of line, then this can result in a disconnect. The small detail I am referring to is how we listened to what God spoke.

When someone speaks to you, you are hearing through the filters of your experience, perspective, opinions, excitements or fears, emotions, pain or wounds, and the condition of your heart. This can cause huge misunderstandings and breakdowns in communication. For the most part, people listen in order to respond. Have you ever noticed yourself listening to someone and being more focused on what you will say in return, how you will argue your case, or how you will convince them that your opinion is right? Our problem is that we too often listen with the intention of responding out of our own agenda and motives, rather than listening attentively.

When we listen to understand, we listen wholeheartedly; we still our minds and silence all the other voices—including our egos. We focus on the words the speaker is saying with intent to understand. We want to grasp the "hows" and "whys" of their perspective on the topic of discussion. This principle is the same when we're listening to God. How else can we grasp the entirety of His message? Even then, we only will get a fragment of the wealth of his intentions for us.

Did you notice in Proverbs that wisdom is a valuable asset to have? One of wisdom's brothers is understanding, which is the correct interpretation of a matter. We all need both wisdom and understanding to humbly listen to God's voice, remembering that we are made from the dust; God is the infinite being who rules the universe.

In this book series, I often refer to the children of Israel's journey from Egypt into Canaan, otherwise known as the land of promise. There are a vast number of lessons to be learned by looking at both the right and wrong decisions they made in the journey. Many people only look to those who seemingly did everything right in their journey as their examples. But the Holy Spirit has taught me over the years to also learn from what others have gotten wrong. Wisdom can be attained from almost any situation; it just depends on what you are looking for and willing to learn.

I have always seen the Israelite's journey from Egypt to Canaan as a type of our lives. There are valuable lessons to be learned so we won't end up dying in the desert. For example, look at the twelve spies. These were twelve men, the finest chosen from the twelve tribes of Israel, who went across the Jordan to boldly spy out the land they had trekked all the way from Egypt to inherit. After the twelve returned from their reconnaissance trip, only two bold men came back with faith; the other ten returned as cowards with no courage to go forward and take the land. It was not going to be an easy walk.

God's promise was for the children of Israel, not for just the two bold men who had faith. The twelve spies who ventured into the land, each had their own individual wills. God had stated His perfect will, which was to give them this territory. From what I have learned in situations where promises are given to more than one individual (churches, friends, business partners, married couples, dating and engaged couples, even territories and nations), the claiming of the promise can be slightly more complex due to the fact that everyone must be in agreement, collectively yielding to God's will.

I have run a couple of companies, and every time we interact with a customer we sign a contract and send an invoice. It outlines in detail what the customer is going to pay and what the company will provide the customer in return. Now if one aspect of that agreement between those two parties is changed, then everything changes. In a similar way, when God gives a promise, we must always remember that there are conditions that accompany that promise.

In the case of the twelve men who spied out the land that was *already* promised to them by God, only Joshua and Caleb believed they could have the land. This was the same God who brought them out of Egypt with plundered silver and gold, parted the Red Sea and then destroyed Pharaoh's army in it. This promise was given by the same God who led them with a cloud by day and a pillar of fire by night, provided manna and water, and who *personally* met Moses on the mountain to give him the Ten Commandments, inscribed with His own hand. The rest of the spies were afraid and seemed to have quickly forgotten all these miracles that God had performed on their short journey thus far. This was the same God who promised to give them the land as their inheritance, a promise passed down since God spoke with Abraham. Now they stood at the river's edge, dipping their hot, dry, dusty feet in the water, looking across to their promised destination, Canaan.

Because *they all* did not agree and align their wills with the will of God, *they all* missed the open door that would take them into the Promised Land the first time. And that door did not open again for forty years! Sometimes these prophetic promises have windows of opportunities that are only available at certain times, much like revolving doors.

The first plan was scrapped and plan B then took its place. God always has a second, third, and fourth plan—at least that's the way we see it. He has never been and never will be caught off guard. He is the most brilliant strategist. The important part is that when God gives us the opportunity, we must enter in. Somehow from eternity, outside of time, God already knows what we will do, and His plans are never foiled.

There are requirements to fulfill your destiny in God's plan. Therefore, we must walk humbly before the Lord. Sometimes God hasn't changed His mind, but we simply have misinterpreted what He said or filled in the blanks before He could show us His real plan. Don't assume anything; walk humbly allowing God to work with you.

Earlier in my life, I met a girl and God spoke to me as clear as day that she would be my wife. In fact, He didn't just speak once; I had multiple visions, Scriptures, and confirmations from others who knew nothing about this girl. I even met her father in a dream before I met him in person; in the dream, he told me all about his daughter. The way he spoke about her in the dream was the same way he talked about her in real life when I met him. I was excited— God was speaking loudly to me! I pursued her with confidence and in time we started dating.

As time progressed, however, she eventually told me, "I won't pay the price to walk down the road God has shown you," even after she had initially said she would. I was not going to compromise what God had spoken to me regarding His plans and destinies. How can two walk together unless they be agreed? But I did not remain single; God shifted me to His plan B. God's plan B is never a second best; in fact, His plan B is always better than His original plan.

For example, in the book of Esther, we read that when Vashti rebelled against the king, the king found someone better. Sometimes

God changes the plan. Because God is not a man, but God, He knew plan B was really plan A the whole time. Sometimes what we believe is plan A is really a test to see if we qualify for the actual promise; God is seeing if we will really trust Him.

If you don't think God does this type of thing, just look at Abraham's son of promise, Isaac. (see Genesis 17:19) It was physically impossible for Abraham and Sarah to have children due to their old age. God took them through an intense journey of waiting and faith, but they finally received their son. He must have been precious to them. However, later God tells Abraham to take Isaac up the mountain, build an altar, and sacrifice his son to God (see Genesis 22). Seems sadistic, right? Well, we know that God allowed him to prepare everything, right up to the point of raising the knife, when the angel of the Lord stayed Abraham's hand and provided an animal to be sacrificed in Isaac's place. Abraham was tested, and as a result of his obedience, God provided a substitute. God was pointing to the day He would send His own Son Jesus to save us from our sin.

Trust Him and always be ready to move with His cloud. God's cloud, that led the children of Israel through the desert away from Egypt and toward the Promised Land, was not the destination. It was a marker, like a breadcrumb trail to be followed. Sometimes we get this mixed up. God is leading us, not telling us to build a house there.

Even though it may appear that God has shifted from plan A to plan B, He is still on plan A. We see it as plan B through our human mind-sets and limited perspectives. God knew what was going to take place all along, even before He made the earth and all that was in it. He knew that Adam and Eve would fall into sin and be separated from His presence, so God prepared a way of redemption. He would send his Son, born of a virgin, to be crucified on a cross, take all our sin upon Himself, and defeat Satan's power of sin and death. That was God's plan A from the beginning—and it was beautiful. Seeing through God's perspective is important in order to understand God as the author of our story.

The Scriptures say that we need to look "unto Jesus, the author and finisher of our faith, who for the joy that was set before Him endured the cross, despising the shame, and has sat down at the right hand of the throne of God" (Hebrews 12:2). God is the scriptwriter of our life's story. In order to stay true to the story, we need to stay in a place of intimacy, listening and maintaining a sensitive spirit so we can see His breadcrumb trail in front of us on the path of life.

Jeremiah 29:11 is God's perspective over us—He has clear and well-planned-out pathways and promises for our lives that He wants us to enjoy. The only way we can experience what God desires for us, is to be lead by His voice and hand throughout the span of our lives. Circumstances and people can interrupt the time-line continuum, but God is not defeated, confused or outwitted. He simply slides in a few variables and engages the next plan, which He foresaw from the beginning. It's in moments like these that we must stay calm and trust that God is in control, and has divine perspective.

It's also important to remember that we won't automatically jump to the final promise of blessing. For instance, let's say God wants to get us to a blessing at point D. From point A, which is where we currently are, point D doesn't look very attractive. So what God does instead is get us to point B because we can handle that. Then, in time, He shifts us to point C, and so forth, until we get to point D.

We must always be open to a change in the plans and leading of God; sometimes we miss God because we block Him out. When God sends a message to shift us from point D, we sometimes reject it because we become sentimental creatures who do not like change. We veer toward tradition. Jesus said to the Pharisees, "[You're] making the word of God of no effect through your tradition which you have handed down" (Mark 7:13). Culture and sentiments can nullify God's ability to move in your life and bless you! We must not be stubborn people as we follow God's leading.

Rather, we must be like the children of Israel who looked up when the cloud or pillar of fire moved and stopped. Take expectations and preconceived ideas out of your planning and become an innocent follower of God's plans. Become childlike in your faith, for God has the right to write the script any way He sees fit. He has the right to change what we think is the plan for our lives! He is the author and finisher of our faith, not we ourselves. It would do us well to trust Him and be obedient to all He asks of us.

CHAPTER 14

HOW TO TEST THE WORD OF THE LORD

God's has the best plan for each of us. His ideal and desirable future for us is both exciting and challenging. One of the greatest enemies, if not the primary nemesis of finding and walking in God's will, is our emotions. There are two main streams in our emotions, the first being the love/lust emotion that draws us toward an object, whether healthy or otherwise; and second is the emotion of fear/doubt that causes us to feel intimidated or even the need to avoid or run.

For example, let's say that God is speaking to you about selling your home, packing up your belongings, and going to a nation that will be difficult to live in. Maybe you hear God tell you this, but you fear abandoning all your earthly possessions, family, and friends; maybe you fear leaving behind the comfortable life you are used to, the food you love and the places you love to go. These emotions can cause you to question what God has spoken and your judgment can become clouded. The emotion of fear is a powerful tool of the devil to distract you from what God has said.

The next issue arises from our own carnal desires. Maybe we want something so strongly, and have not even asked God about it. Perhaps we have even overridden God's voice. At times we can even talk ourselves into believing that what we want, is what God wants. This is dangerous, because it is a self-generated leading motivated by feelings. We can sell ourselves like used car salesmen on words that in truth, God has not spoken at all.

This is seen in the life of Samson. God had specifically instructed him to be a chaste Nazarite and to marry a daughter of Israel. Instead he ended up in Delilah's lap and thus lost his strength. Lust is a strong desire for something that does not belong to you. When we allow lust to consume our minds, it creates the delusion that what we are wanting is in God's plan. Every Christian has done this at least once and has the scars to prove it. Scars are powerful reminders never to do *that* again. Lust was the tool the devil used in the garden with Adam and Eve. Lust is a strong desire and an appeal for something that God has clearly forbidden.

We must return to Jeremiah 29:11 to see that God only has the best intentions for us, and ultimately, He will give us a far better outcome than anything we can try to get for ourselves on our own. Again, heeding the advice of Proverbs is helpful here: "Trust in the LORD with all your heart, lean not on your own understanding, in all your ways acknowledge Him, and He will direct your paths" (Proverbs 3:5–6). God leads us by His Spirit when we submit to Him.

This is one of the reasons we must enter the kingdom as little children. Children are less polluted in their thinking and accept things they are told much more readily than most adults. Hearing God speak and readily receiving it in a childlike way is the safest place to live and walk with God.

To be sure of God's will and not be deceived, we must become like Gideon. He was a righteous man, and after the Angel of the Lord appeared to him, he still wanted God to confirm His word. Many people look at Gideon at this stage of his life in a slightly negative way in that he waited around and tested God three times to make sure he heard correctly. Instead of jumping straight into action, he waited for God to confirm what He had asked of him. Gideon was a wise man who absolutely wanted to be sure that he had heard from God. I admire his persistence to return to the God of heaven and earth three times and continue to ask until there was no doubt in his mind. After that, he was a solid rock and went out grounded in the word of the Lord.

There is added confidence in the heart when we know what God has spoken. There is no room for the devil to challenge God's word. A person convinced they have heard God becomes unmovable and unstoppable. "Now it came to pass, when the time had come for [Jesus] to be received up, that He steadfastly set His face to go to Jerusalem" (Luke 9:51). Jesus had heard the Father. He knew what awaited Him in Jerusalem, and He understood the Father's plan. In the flesh, it was not an appealing plan, yet he was determined not to bow to any devilish scheme to abandon His road to the cross—even when it came from His close friend.

There's an old saying that says, "Stand for something or fall for anything." Hearing God's voice is similar. Jesus said, "My sheep listen to my voice; I know them, and they follow me" (John 10:27 NIV). It is imperative to *know* what God has said to you. If you don't know, then don't be hasty in any decision-making, as it could likely be the wrong one.

Knowing what God has said will cause you to quickly identify counterfeit leadings, opportunities, and even the appearance of open doors. If you don't know what God has said or is saying to you, then stop and seek Him. Do not move until you are certain.

TEST ALL THINGS

It is often quoted that Satan can appear as an angel of light (see 2 Corinthians 11:14). He is constantly looking to derail us because he is the enemy of our souls. He is a wolf in sheep's clothing. The devil's voice will appeal to your emotions and paint a picture that most of the time will be the easier option. If you cannot judge what God is saying, then it's time to test the spirits.

As I mentioned, my number one rule is never to be hasty in moving toward something until I really know it is from God. If we are not sure, then we need to think about it like unopened mail—it arrived at your house, but you need to take a closer look at it to determine what it is. Don't get carried away by your emotions and get on a fast-track course in the wrong direction. Testing something that you think may be God is the wisest choice you could ever make. Ask yourself these questions:

1. Does this line up with every relevant Scripture in the Bible—not just the one Scripture that people take out of context to justify their intent, but with the whole counsel of God's Word?

2. Does this line up with all the previous words that God has given me for this area of my life?

3. How is my relationship with God right now?

The reason to ask yourself this third question is that so many people in my life have been in bad places in their walk with God, yet out of nowhere say that God told them to do something. It is impossible to argue with "God said," and that is why we must carefully and humbly keep a close relationship with God. I have seen people make these huge "God-said" statements only to turn back around in a radically different direction using another "God-said" statement as their explanation.

I have watched countless people walk away from their God-given callings, God-given relationships, and followed their "God-said" pathways down roads that are far different from where God was leading them. It is virtually impossible to convince someone once they have committed to this "new and exciting" path. People leave the places of fellowship God has planted them in, using these excuses. The root is usually an offense that needed a reason to move away, and eventually their strong wills manufactured a "God-said" statement.

I have heard *genuine* "God-said" statements, but they come at a price; they require a higher and more challenging road to be walked. "Then Jesus said to His disciples, 'If anyone desires to come after Me, let him deny himself, and take up his cross, and follow Me'" (Matthew 16:24). Here we find a true picture of following the plans of God. The problem is that today we live in a world where everyone wants comfort, luxury, and the easy road of Christianity. But make no mistake about it—that is not Christianity.

1. What do my spiritual parents or pastors think of what I am hearing? What's their input? Never be too proud to have someone wiser and more mature than you speak into your life and assess certain leadings and decisions.

2. Is there a genuine peace over this? If you feel any tension at all, a strained pressure or anxiety, or if you are feeling rushed or hasty in your spirit, then this may not be God who is speaking to you.

3. How much time have I invested into seeking God about this? Five minutes might not be enough!

4. What have I been asking God? Have you been asking Him, "Will You let me have?" or have you been asking, "What do You want?" These are two different questions. The first is loaded and pressured, like a child asking for ice cream; the second is humble and submitted.

THE WORD OF GOD

God's Word will always back up authentic prophetic revelation. There is no extra-biblical revelation, which is why we must daily immerse ourselves in the Word of God. Having a sound grasp on the words of the Bible will give us accurate perspective on God's ways. John writes, "The Spirit, the water and the blood; and the three are in agreement" (1 John 5:8 NIV). To put it more simply, the Spirit of God has different functions, one of them being the prophetic, and He will *never* disagree with the Word of God. This means that no dream, vision, word from the Lord or leading from the Spirit will ever contradict the written Word of God. God is not confused nor is He the author of confusion.

Don't be fooled into thinking you are the exception and have a unique situation where God will make an allowance. Jesus did not bend the rules to avoid the cross; He was obedient to the Word of God, and I will be forever grateful for His sacrifice and obedience. People go wrong when they search for one Scripture they can creatively interpret to fit their desired "leading." I tend to reference 2 Corinthians 13:1, which states, "In the mouth of two or three witnesses shall every word be established." I use at least two or three Scriptures, in their correct contexts, to confirm that what I am feeling God is showing me is in fact, scriptural.

As an example, if an unmarried couple who are dating started to say that God had "released" them to have sex outside of being married, and that God had made an exception for them, I would have to ask, "Does this line up with the Word of God?" or "What Scriptures are there that talk about this?" It will quickly become obvious that God commands us not to have sex outside of marriage. It seems simple, but too many Christians are caught in deceptions like these because they do not know the Word of God! God said, "My people are destroyed for lack of knowledge" (Hosea 4:6). If you get any knowledge at all, then get it from the Bible!

IS IT ANOINTED?

If you have been intimately walking with God for a while, you will become familiar with His presence and His anointing. I have found that when I pray, if there is no presence or anointing when I am asking Him for something, then generally I will continue to seek Him while choosing my questions wisely. If there continues to be no presence, then I will consider that God isn't in it. Therefore, I won't pursue it.

Spend less time reasoning, and spend more time talking to your heavenly Father about it. Stay calm and give God the opportunity to reveal the path. Praying opens the channels to God's throne as you humbly submit to Him. I love looking at the Lord's Prayer as a model:

> *Our Father who lives in heaven [you are identifying God for who He really is],*

> *Hallowed be your name [holy and honored is His name, which puts Him on the throne].*

Your kingdom come, Your will be done [this changes perspective from the earthly kingdom and our wills being done and placing God as the focal point],

On earth as it is in heaven [you are asking God's world to enter your world].

Give us this day our daily bread [God is our provider, so we must see Him that way. We don't have the responsibility or ability to take care of our own needs].

Forgive us our trespasses as we forgive those that trespass against us [seeing Father God as the one who has the power to forgive us of our sins, and that we in turn must forgive those who sin against us and kneel at the throne in humility].

Lead us not into temptation, but deliver us from evil [there is a clear reliance on the protection and care of God here].

For Yours is the kingdom, the power and the glory for ever and ever, amen [this is the ultimate exultation of God our Father. He is the greatest, the most powerful King of the universe!].

The beginning of the prayer opens with a reverent acknowledgement of who God the Father is, and shows Him great honor and respect. I have learned that honor and respect is essential to growing my relationship with Father God. Then the prayer progresses toward preferring God's will, plan, and kingdom over our own. Then the requests start. First, provision, then repentance and forgiveness of others, and the request to be forgiven. Then the request to be protected and covered. Finally, exalting God for who He is.

This was the formula given by Jesus in Matthew 6:9–13, and I want to pray like that. Never order God around; He is not your personal genie in a bottle, or your waiter, only here to serve your every whim and desire. Don't ever treat God like that because He only wants your heart and to be in relationship with you. From there, He can take care of your desires, needs, and requests!

Again, be like Gideon and ask God for signs and confirmations until you are undoubtedly satisfied that you really know what God is saying. When I was asking God about my wife, before I married her, I asked if she was the one He had for me. I spent a great deal of time seeking Him. God gave me multiple dreams, visions, and Scriptures and aside from that, He spoke to me specifically. Seeking God over time, He painted me a picture of His perfect will.

If you doubt the word you have received, then shelve it for later. Time reveals all truth. If you are unsure of something that could or could not be from God, wait and leave it for later. There is no rush! Let God reveal the real plan to you in His time.

CHECKING PROPHETIC WORDS

It's important to stop and make sure that what you are hearing, sensing, or seeing is inspired by God and not just your imagination. Take the time to confirm that you have the full picture of what He is saying and not just a partial understanding. I will always stop what I am doing when He is showing me something, and double or even triple check with Him to make sure I am hearing right. Verify with God; don't be hasty to jump to conclusions. Here are a few ways God can confirm to us that we are hearing Him.

I will always wait to see that the tangible presence of God rests on me as I am receiving the word of the Lord from Him. This bears witness with the word of the Lord. Sometimes we will feel the peace of God, while at other times we experience His fire and power burning or pulsating in and around us. Ask God to pour out His presence or withhold it when you are assessing a prophecy. Absence of presence usually means absence of God's agreement.

The Scriptures tell us that signs follow the preaching of the Word. (see Mark 16:7–18) God is not afraid to back up His word with signs that confirm that what is being said is really from Him. Ask God to give you signs to confirm this word. Often, in my personal experience, these signs will come in the form of dreams.

Dreams are a phenomenal avenue God uses to speak and confirm His word. He often uses dreams because we are not distracted, and we can perceive the spirit realm more easily. No one can take credit for these moments; God chooses to divinely deliver revelation in this way. Many times, God will confirm to us the things He has been saying while we are awake. Always discern the source of your dreams as the enemy can use this avenue at times too. Ask God to speak to you and confirm His voice in your dreams.

I have had a few encounters with angels who were sent to confirm various messages that God had been speaking to me about. These moments were powerful and impacting. Just like dreams though, you must be discerning, as the Word of God instructs us to "test the spirits" (see 1 John 4:1). We must discern which spiritual camp each visitation is coming from so we are not deceived or misled. Do not be afraid of these encounters; ask God to use angels to confirm His messages to you.

The prophetic will never contradict the written Word of God. You must study the Word of God, consuming it until it becomes your inner compass. Measure everything by the benchmark of the Word. Reject any prophetic word that does not agree 100 percent with the Bible. Ask the Holy Spirit to train you to grow strong in the Word of God, so you can immediately identify the source of each message that is spoken. But, most importantly, test the word of the Lord.

CHAPTER 15

RECOGNIZING YOUR PROMISE

There is something profound about a long-awaited dream being realized and inherited! Doesn't food taste better after a long, hard day at work? Realizing a prophetic promise after a long period of believing, praying, sowing, waiting, and waiting some more is such a sweet blessing. When you get to your destination, you are more equipped and more prepared than you were when God first spoke to you about it.

We read of Joseph, who was the grandson of Abraham, in the book of Genesis. When Joseph was a young boy, he had amazing dreams of his future destiny. But he had no idea of the journey that would he would have to make. He did not realize he was about to embark on an abrasive series of events. Joseph was rejected, thrown into a pit by his brothers and sold into slavery to his cultural enemies. From there, he was further sold into Egypt and purchased by a man named Potiphar. Joseph grew in favor and eventually managed Potiphar's house. Then more disaster struck. He was accused by

Potiphar's wife, who unsuccessfully attempted to seduce him. He refused her advances, she subsequently accused him anyway, and he was thrown in prison and forgotten for fourteen years. In the prison, Scripture tells us:

> *They hurt his feet with fetters,*
>
> *He was laid in irons.*
>
> *Until the time that his word came to pass,*
>
> *The word of the LORD tested him. (Psalm 105:18–19)*

God equips and prepares us in the journey. During these hardships, Joseph continued to walk before God with a right heart, and he continued to steward his gifts. In fact, he interpreted dreams for both the baker and the cupbearer, and because of their accuracy, he was remembered and released from prison in order to interpret Pharaoh's dreams.

It wasn't until after he had interpreted Pharaoh's dreams and the famine broke out that he began to see the destiny given to him as a boy unfold. Joseph went from dreams, to betrayal, to slavery, to accusation, to prison, to liberation from his cell, to promotion into Pharaoh's courts, and into his destiny as prime minister of all of Egypt, eventually saving his entire family. The journey, although not an easy one, was the preparation he needed for his destination. What is profound is that the cocky young boy who had the grandiose dreams as a child, became the man who stood and wept as his brothers bowed before him. He wept because he saw his brothers, but he also wept as he realized the crazy dream from so long ago, had come to pass.

The process had changed him; he was not bitter and hateful. Realization of his childhood dreams had confirmed that his journey had ultimately fulfilled the plan of God for not only his life, but for the lives of his family as well. It was not just the dregs of a bad series of events.

In a similar way David received an anointing poured out from Samuel's flask of oil to indicate that the Lord had elected him as the next king of Israel. David had killed a lion and a bear defending his father's flock of sheep, these victories were big in their own right, but when viewed in the big picture of his life story, they were only a part of his training process. David held fast to the promise God gave him through Samuel—he had been chosen to be king over Israel. It was a powerful promise from the most credible prophet in all of Israel, but David needed to walk wisely to inherit it.

The day that David walked onto the battlefield to bring his brothers lunch and heard the roaring taunts of the giant Goliath, the champion of the Philistine army, he also heard of the reward for killing him. Just imagine, the second David heard about the reward, he realized it could be a doorway into the king's courts, and an opportunity that would lead him closer to his destiny. He also recognized the enormous challenge he would face coming against the enemy of God's chosen people. I love and admire the boldness in David. We see from the time Samuel anointed David as the future king of Israel that he began to believe that his destiny was exactly as Samuel had said, and God's dream became his own. David owned it and it began to transform him. The long-awaited dream was realized.

The journey you have walked has likely trained you to walk worthy of your destination. Remember that God has planned your journey, and although you have been trained by the highs and the lows, there is more learning and equipping ahead. You will need to walk and talk in wisdom and integrity before the Lord and others. The slightest hint of pride and arrogance will be a blockage, hindering your ministry and keeping you from fulfilling the role God has given you. Don't miss the sometimes humble package that your promise may arrive in. Do you realize the Jewish people waited for the prophesied Messiah, avidly watching for decades, even centuries, and then did not recognize Jesus as the fulfillment of the promise even as He stood and taught right in front of them?

You may be required to step out of your "safe waiting place" in order to enter your inheritance. This is risky. This is much like David speaking up in the presence of his brothers and the King and like Peter getting out of the safety of the boat with the other disciples and walking on the water with Jesus. Stepping out is often risky, awkward, and uncomfortable. But the reward of arriving at the promise is worth it. God takes such a deep pleasure when we operate in faith. Our faith is strengthened to take on new challenges and obtain further promises and offered to God as a pleasing gift.

I was talking to some pastor friends recently, and they were sharing their story of how they were called to lead a church. As they stepped out to lead, they found they needed to resign from their stable, good paying jobs in order to do what God called them to do. Before making a radical decision like they did, they had to be positive that they had heard God and double-checked that it was in fact Him.

This wonderful couple went on to share that it was difficult at first and it really stretched them, but in good time, they were given a nice house. In addition, they were given a large sum of money to fund the church. If God sends you, then He is going to provide, even though it might not happen quickly or easily. We need to face struggles with confidence, hanging on to His word through the transition from comfort to the unknown. This is why the writer of Hebrews tells us, "And without faith it is impossible to please God, because anyone who comes to Him must believe that He exists and that he rewards those who earnestly seek Him" (Hebrews 11:6 NIV). And God tells us, "Do not despise these small beginnings, for the LORD rejoices to see the work begin" (Zechariah 4:10 NLT).

Sometimes we imagine a destiny of grandeur, but often God's path for our lives is the unattractive road and the less-obvious option. God's way is the way of humility. It cannot be forced by our own abilities and ambitions. Proverbs reminds us, "The fear of the LORD is instruction in wisdom, and humility comes before honor" (Proverbs 15:33 ESV).

HOW TO LOOK FOR YOUR PROMISE

Always remember what God promised you initially. That's why the Lord told Habakkuk to write the promise down and send a runner. It is important that the promise stay true to the original version—without changing. Write down and record the promises of God so you can recall exactly what was given and their exact interpretation. This is important because, as you get closer to the realization of the promise, greater understanding will be revealed and more clarity given.

God is so wise, and He will often hide some of the details in His statements in plain sight. The book of Revelation, for example, is much better understood by this generation today than the generation that came immediately after the apostle John. God told John to "seal up the word" or make the message cryptic, so that it would not be understood till the appointed time. This can be true for us personally as our journey gets closer to the destination. Continually reminding ourselves of the promises keeps us focused on our inheritance.

God will reveal the promised destination in His own way. Be open to Him. If we have preconceived ideas of what it's supposed to look like or how it is supposed to play out, then it can lead us to reject God's opportunities when they present themselves. This is one of the reasons why many of the Jews rejected Jesus as the Messiah when He was on the earth. They were looking for something they had fabricated in their minds rather than being open to God's ways.

Be desperate and anticipate the promise, but never get so negatively desperate that you are prepared to settle for anything less.

You're going to have to step out in faith! Pay attention to the children of Israel who were in slavery for over four hundred years and then were liberated by the strong hand of God. When it came time to cross over from their season of waiting into their season of possessing the promise, they choked up and wouldn't step out in faith because of fear. While we wait, positioned in sometimes awkward in-between places, we need to remember that there will be a time when we will shift into an inheriting stance. It will likely be unfamiliar and uncomfortable. We cannot afford to doubt or refuse to open the door when it is time to transition.

Once you see the door of God's promise opening, it's time to carefully consult with God that this is in fact His plan for your life, not a distraction. Once you are certain, it's time to boldly and confidently walk into your inheritance, knowing you are fully equipped. It's time to receive your promise!

A WORD TO THE READER

The material that you have just read is essential for your growth and development; allow it to soak into your mind and spirit. Establish your walk with God by these principles we discussed. People have all sorts of opinions about how we should live and walk with Him, but there can only be one way authored by God.

God's methods do not change. In an increasingly fast-paced world where technology trains us to become accustomed to instant everything, it is difficult to let God work on His timetable and be patient while we wait for the fulfillment of God's promises. Don't let the world's desire for instant gratification make you impatient. God does not need to reinvent Himself; rather, we need to bend to His ways. Submit to God; be entirely dependent on Him as your source. He is the architect of every detail of your life. There is incredible beauty and blessing when we walk in harmony with God's will.

Remember, your life is a process and the details of each specific prophetic promise are important. Find God's fingerprints in your story and follow Him as closely as you can. If you follow the advice found in this volume, you will inherit the promises of God.

As a growing prophet, trust God to equip you to become a trustworthy mouthpiece of the Lord. God has called you for such a time as this; people may be waiting for you to walk in the fullness of your destiny.

THE PROPHETIC TRAINING SERIES:

VOL. I — THE FOUNDATIONS OF THE PROPHETIC

VOL. II — THE PROCESS OF THE PROPHETIC

VOL. III — THE OFFICE OF THE PROPHET

VOL. IV — THE EQUIPMENT OF THE PROPHET

VOL. V — THE PITFALLS OF THE PROPHETIC

VOL. VI — THE ESSENTIALS OF THE PROPHET

VOL. VII — THE NEMESIS OF THE PROPHET

Order the series today and receive a discounted package price. Please follow us on Facebook and sign up for e-mail updates about upcoming books and events at www.AndrewBillings.org or www.GuildOfTheProphets.com.

Guild of the Prophets School—Coming Soon.

JOIN THE GUILD OF THE PROPHETS

Prophets need prophets; in fact, we should not isolate ourselves from others in the prophetic community. I want to encourage you to sign up and join the Guild of the Prophets. In joining the Guild, you will be encouraged, strengthened, and informed of additional prophetic resources, special pricing, and limited-access events that may be of interest to you. Membership is free.

Look out for the other titles coming soon in the Guild of the Prophets series. This prophetic equipping series has been designed as a school of the prophets, meant to help you grow, develop, and mature into the fullness of your calling in this amazing ministry of expressing God's heart to the world. The Guild of the Prophets books are available for purchase at:

ANDREWBILLINGS.ORG

GUILDOFTHEPROPHETS.COM

At the age of twenty-one, while running away from God, Andrew Billings had a powerful encounter while working as a project manager in Bora Bora, in the islands of Tahiti. While Andrew slept one night, two large, seven-foot angels dressed in white robes with golden belts came into his room and took him in the spirit to a place where He had a personal encounter with Jesus. During that encounter, Andrew experienced the love and mercy of God in ways He had not seen while growing up in church. Jesus walked Him through His entire life's history, giving him a glimpse of being condemned to hell if he did not yield his whole life into God's hands. Jesus went on to show Andrew the future of his life in an open vision, and asked him to help Him save many. That moment was a pivotal point in Andrew's walk with God.

Since that time, Andrew has had many such encounters. His desire is to see many set on fire with passion for the Lord, and to raise up a generation of those who want to experience all God offers. His heart is to see heaven populated with those who have been impacted by the glory and power of God flowing through others.

··· NEXT IN THE SERIES ···

GUILD OF THE PROPHETS

THE OFFICE

OF THE PROPHET

VOL.

III

YOU WILL LEARN ABOUT:

1 — THE HEART AND MOTIVES AND CHARACTERISTICS OF A PROPHET.

2 — YOUR SCHOOLING & PREPARATION PROCESS AS A PROPHET.

3 — TUNING INTO YOUR UNIQUE HEARING CHANNEL.

4 — ESSENTIAL WISDOM & SPEAKING AS AN ORACLE.

5 — WHAT EVERY CHURCH LEADER WANTS YOU TO KNOW.

6 — UNDERSTANDING AND WALKING IN PROPHETIC CREATIVITY.

7 — WHAT DOES A PROPHETS MINISTRY AND JOB DESCRIPTION LOOK LIKE?